THE ILLUMINATI
GATEWAY

Ascension Initiation

Keys for Higher Evolution

Michael Garber

Copyright © 2022
MICHAEL GARBER
THE ILLUMINATION CODEX
All rights reserved.

No part of this publication may be reproduced, distributed, or transmitted in any form or by any means, including photocopying, recording, or other electronic or mechanical methods, without the prior written permission of the publisher, except in the case of brief quotations embodied in critical reviews and certain other non-commercial uses permitted by copyright law.

MICHAEL GARBER

Printed in the United States of America
First Printing 2021
First Edition 2021

Second Edition

ISBNs:
Softcover 978-1-959561-03-3
eBook 978-1-959561-04-0

10 9 8 7 6 5 4 3 2 1

The Illumination Codex

Table of Contents

ACKNOWLEDGMENTS 7
DEDICATION AND INVOCATION 9
GUIDANCE FOR READING THIS BOOK 11
ABOUT THE AUTHOR 17
    Awakening to the Quantum Reality 17
NEW EARTH ASCENDING VISIONARY CREED 27
GATEWAY ONE: Ascension Initiation 31
    Keys for Higher Evolution 31
    ONE: The Shift of the Ages 33
    TWO: Earth School Orientation 44
    THREE: The Human Experience 54
    FOUR: High Alchemy of the Soul 68
    FIVE: Awakening in the Matrix 77
    SIX: Universal Laws of Creation 90
    SEVEN: Ascension and Descension Cycles of Consciousness 101
    EIGHT: Ascension Symptom Care 108
    NINE: Shifting to New Earth 115
    TEN: Family of Light Blessing 134
    ELEVEN: Manifestation of New Earth Prayer 140

Ascension Lexicon 143
Recommended Reading 163
Support Our Initiatives 165

ACKNOWLEDGMENTS

I bow in humble recognition of the One Light of Consciousness, the Source of my being and the source of all knowledge and wisdom. I give gratitude to the Supreme for dreaming me into existence and allowing me to have the conscious experience of life and the crafting of this codex.

I bow in love and gratitude to my dear beloved partner Ron Amit, a true gift of the Divine, for all the many ways he supports me in my life. I am blessed beyond measure to have such a brilliant master of love, compassion, and divine service to walk this earthly life with. Thank you for all that you do, seen and unseen, to amplify joy and higher consciousness for me and all beings in the Cosmos. I love you across all space, time, and dimensions.

I send gratitude to my friends and clients who have brought forth the lost stories of Creation through their Illuminated Quantum Healing hypnosis sessions. Thank you for being the powerful Light beacons that you are!

I send deep gratitude to my many modern scribes who assisted me in the transcription work. Thank you for helping me capture these incredible client stories so that the world can remember our cosmic divine heritage.

Bless all the beings, seen and unseen, who have helped me craft this material so that you, the reader, can be nourished on your path of Ascension. May you, the reader, be blessed infinitely and discover the highest truth of your being. May ascended consciousness, liberation, and divine unification be yours in this very life!

DEDICATION AND INVOCATION

This book is dedicated to the infinite expressions of our Oneself, for the celebration of our many incarnations, past, present, and future, and the lessons we have learned throughout eternity. May these words and the energy they carry be a potent force for awakening for all seekers of Unconditional Love and divine Truth. May this transmission support the reactivation and restoration of humanity's divine blueprint upon planet Earth and accelerate the realization of our eternal unity and oneness with all of Creation.

Let us join in prayer, honoring and sending gratitude to the Supreme Intelligent Source of Creation, the omniscient, omnipotent, omnipresent, transcendental Divine Source that is our True Nature.

Let us honor and send gratitude to the higher Light realms and the beings of Light who guide and protect Creation's evolution. Let us honor and send gratitude to our star lineages and those who support us from beyond the Earth. Let us receive your love and blessings now as we remember our cosmic ancestry and our role in the higher evolutionary plan for Creation.

Let us honor and send gratitude to our Earth Mother and her many dimensions and manifestations of Life including the animal, plant, bacterial, fungal, protozoan, mineral, crystalline, and elemental beings who contribute to her dynamic, regenerative biomes. These writings are offered as salve and balm to heal and bless our beloved Gaia, our Earth Mother and Divine Sister. May her waters be pure, her soil rich, her air clean, and may all beings, seen and unseen, within her living biofield know lasting peace forever and ever.

Let us honor and send gratitude to the wisdom and guidance from the seven directions of East, South, West, North, Above, Below, and Within. Let us call back our soul fragments scattered through time and space so that we may anchor ourselves HERE and NOW in this eternal moment of infinite potential to witness the unfolding manifestation of the Divine Plan.

Let us honor and send gratitude to the elements of Earth, Air, Fire, Water, and Ether that create the foundation of our evolutionary experience in form. May the Light of Consciousness awaken swiftly in each of us as we remember our True Nature beyond names and forms.

Let us honor and send gratitude to our ancestors and the many souls who have shared their light upon the Earth. Let us send special thanks to those who dedicated their lives to passing on the Mysteries and sacred knowledge of the Divine so that we may NOW stand at this Grand Turning of the Ages, with the support of all who have come and all who are destined to live upon this great Earth.

I call forth the full remembering of our divinity and the weaving of a new story of harmony and peace for all of Life upon the Earth. May we shed our stories of limitation and suffering and step forward into a new era as People of Light, cosmic co-citizens, and ambassadors for the Living Light of Creation.

Hallelujah! Jai! Aho! Blessed Be! Amen! And so, it is! Om!

GUIDANCE FOR READING THIS BOOK

The Illumination Codex is a multidimensional library for the path of Ascension. It is holographic by nature as each chapter contains a multitude of keycodes to activate ancient cellular memory and trigger multidimensional awareness and higher consciousness integration. As you read the material, your Inner Being will offer flashes of insight and higher perception into your awareness to assist you in healing, spiritual activation, and cosmic remembrance. I recommend using a highlighter, journaling your process, and using other resources to research and enhance your understanding of the topics presented in this book.

A major influence for this material comes from my work as a past-life regression hypnotherapist using the methods we have codified into a technique called Illuminated Quantum Healing (IQH). While in a deep hypnotic trance, my clients experience other lifetimes and other planetary civilizations and communicate with advanced intelligent species from beyond the Earth and Earth plane. The information contained in this book is a summary of my understanding of all that I have learned through my clients as they journeyed to the ancient past, probable timelines of the future, and higher planes of Light. There are many transcriptions of IQH sessions included in the book for you to have your own unique interpretation and multidimensional experience with the material.

This book contains a diverse collection of spiritual information from a variety of wisdom traditions that I have studied in my life. These writings are my own interpretations and understandings of these different concepts that have helped me in my awakening journey and do not necessarily speak for the lineages themselves. This presentation of information is meant as a collection of keys to unlock the wisdom that is already encoded within you. None of it is meant to become dogmatic as consciousness revelation and ascendency will open us continuously to higher and higher truths and understanding.

I confess that I share this transmission as a fellow traveler on the path of awakening. I have my own limitations, my own egoic nature, and my own struggles. I am capable of error and ignorance just as any other person. This presentation of information is what I have found along my path which has triggered awakening and helped me on my path back home to my Self. My prayer is that this book will become deeply meaningful for you and be a guiding light back to your own liberated being.

While reading this material, you may come across something in the text that triggers something within you that is uncomfortable. Maybe it is words that I use, perspectives that I share, or something else that may bring up resistance, judgment, anger, guilt, and so on. This is a wonderful opportunity to investigate the origin of the reactive mental and emotional patterns that create such experiences. The origin may come from earlier stages of your life or previous lifetimes. Use this as an opportunity to reconcile those parts of your consciousness through spiritual inquiry and self-study so that you may realize deeper states of wholeness and clarity.

This text is intended to activate 'gnosis,' a direct experience and knowledge of the divine presence within and around you. I do not recommend blind faith in any concept or religious doctrine. The information in this book is not meant to be treated as religious dogma that cannot be questioned or developed further. It is meant to be utilized to unlock the truth that lives within your very being. I am not writing this intending to change people's beliefs or convert anyone. I am simply relaying the summary of my life's research on the quest for spiritual truth. If something from the material does not resonate as truth in your heart, release it and move on to the next part of the transmission. Use the philosophy and information in this text to stimulate your expansion and the embodiment of YOUR deepest truth and to strengthen your relationship and innate connection with the Divine.

Another thing to mention is capitalization. You will notice that there are words that are not normally capitalized in other books and sacred texts that are capitalized in this text. My intention behind this was to add spiritual dimensionality to words that describe qualities or names of the Divine.

Typically, when I speak of light in this book, I am speaking about higher-dimensional, intelligently-encoded subtle energy and not conventional light from a light bulb. When I speak about "energy," I am speaking about subtle energy which exists beyond the visible light spectrum for most people. Many are becoming sensitive to subtle energy (i.e., multisensory, intuitive, psychic) and are developing the ability to sense and perceive this energy through extrasensory perception. All of humanity is evolving towards being able to perceive and interact with subtle energy and higher cosmic intelligence and consciousness.

The use of the term consciousness fluctuates throughout the book and can mean different things. When I speak of pure Consciousness I am speaking about your True Self as Source Consciousness, the Absolute, the Eternal Witness of all Creation, pure Awareness and Existence itself. Other times I will speak of consciousness as in variations of the mind such as unity consciousness or separation consciousness. All forms of consciousness, all experiences of the mind, borrow existence from the One Light of Consciousness and you are that!

I tried my best to organize this text in a way that can be read from front to back like any regular book, but it can also be read any way you feel intuitively called to read it. Part of the reason for the size of this codex is because it is difficult to explain one part without understanding many other components. In my effort to answer all potential and probable questions about ascension, I wrote everything I could on this multifaceted, multidimensional topic.

As you make your journey through this material, there are three stages to help integrate the information and use it to fuel your awakening to your True Nature:

Stage One: Listening (*Sravana*) As you read or listen to the material in this book, allow it to penetrate deeply and work with your inner philosophical understanding. Listen deeply to your Inner Being for there will be flashes of insight and knowing that emerge within your inner consciousness space.

Stage Two: Reflection (*Manana*) Try your best to understand the information contained in this book through self-inquiry and inner philosophical pondering. I am not asking for you to blindly believe any of this transmission. Think of this information as an active hypothesis. You do not have to believe it, but you can reflect over the information and see how it applies to your life.

Stage Three: Integration/Meditation (*Nididhyasana*) As you take in the words in stage one and convert the words to knowledge and understanding in stage two, you move into conviction and integration of knowledge in stage three as you crystalize and embody the Self-knowledge of "I am Pure Consciousness." As you go about your daily life, use the knowledge you have gained to interrupt habit and conditioned thought and re-direct your mind toward the Light of Consciousness that you are.

Gateways of Entry

Besides reading front-to-back or intuitively hopping around, I have created six gateways for you to enter the presentation of the material. I have created one large book that has all of the Illumination Codex material and separated the material into separately published volumes to make the information more digestible. The Gateways are as follows:

GATEWAY ONE: ASCENSION INITIATION: KEYS FOR HIGHER EVOLUTION gives an overall understanding of Ascension, reincarnation, universal law, and a theoretical and philosophical framework concerning Cosmic Evolution. This is an excellent place to start if you are open and eager to learn about these subjects and awakening, you may want to start in Gateway Three.

GATEWAY TWO: AKASHIC DATABASE contains a wide variety of Illuminated Quantum Healing session transcriptions describing key figures and events in the history of Creation, galactic history, ancient planetary history, and probable future timelines of New Earth from clients in hypnotic visionary states. This is a suitable place to enter the material if you already have a general understanding of multidimensionality, galactic civilizations, and the process of personal and planetary ascension. This gateway is conveniently separated into QUANTUM ORIGINS, COSMIC CHRIST TRANSMISSIONS, and NEW EARTH TRANSMISSIONS. If you find yourself resistant to those ideas and are new to these subjects. I recommend developing a meditation practice parallel to reading this material as the transcripts are deeply activating on multiple levels.

GATEWAY THREE: PATH OF AWAKENING: KEYS FOR TRANSFIGURATION is an in-depth collection of spiritual and philosophical wisdom to support personal, relational, and planetary healing. If you are in the beginning stages of awakening or moving through a deep healing process, you may wish to start here so you can develop your consciousness and prepare your mind and body for higher level initiation into the Mysteries.

GATEWAY FOUR: CHAKRA YOGA DISCOURSE transmits deeper

insight into the themes and physio-psycho-spiritual domains of the vortices of life force and perception called the *chakras*. Each section transmits valuable information to understand the common distortions in these processing centers and how to activate and reconcile each center.

GATEWAY FIVE: LAYING HANDS: REIKI & BEYOND is a full manual for learning the art of the laying of hands for healing. The manual clearly describes all the stages, steps, and practices to perform powerfully transformative hands-on-healing sessions for yourself, others, and even in groups. This manual would be acceptable for any Level 1 and Level 2 Reiki course.

GATEWAY SIX: ASCENSION LEXICON is a glossary of commonly used words to describe the process of awakening and ascension. These definitions act as keycode activators to unlock deeper meaning and inner wisdom. Many words used in spiritual/ascension circles are convoluted and sometimes lose their impact because they are misused or misunderstood. I may use words in a way you are not familiar with, or I may use words differently than you. I tried my best to make a glossary with foundational vocabulary to assist with understanding the material. You may wish to read the ASCENSION LEXICON before journeying through the main text of the book.

Bless you on your personal path through this material. May the light in your heart guide you with ease and grace on your journey of initiation with *The Illumination Codex*.

ABOUT THE AUTHOR
Awakening to the Quantum Reality

In the Summer of 2016, I was given a book that forever changed my life's direction called *The Three Waves of Volunteers and the New Earth* by Dolores Cannon. This book was a huge catalyst in my spiritual awakening. Reading the text stirred something deep within me and resonated profoundly with my heart's truth. The book's pages sent waves of energy down my spine as I began to awaken to a higher consciousness reality and remember my purpose for being born upon the Earth at this time.

Dolores Cannon was a world-renowned hypnotherapist specializing in past-life regression. To understand the power of regressive hypnosis, we also need to understand the workings of the mind. The mind can be separated into three categories: the conscious mind, the subconscious mind, and the superconscious mind.

The conscious mind is the ego/personality part of the mind. This active part of the mind uses limited information from the environment and past experiences to make decisions and take care of the body.

The subconscious mind is the recording device of our mind. It records incredible amounts of information at every moment. We easily pull data from the subconscious when we think about something from our past as we access memory.

Deeper in the subconscious, sometimes called the unconscious mind, we have unconscious memories and information, including societal conditioning, painful traumas from this life that are too painful to remember, and memories from other lifetimes. Even though this information is not in the conscious mind, it silently influences our day-to-day experience as reactive emotional momentum, called *samskaras* in Sanskrit, from past events which overlay and filter our experience of the present moment. These subconscious patterns are like applications running in the background of smartphones that quietly drain the processing speed and battery, silently influencing processor speed and functionality.

The superconscious mind is a higher mind capacity that gives us access to intuitive information, extrasensory perception, non-local consciousness, creative genius, universal connection, and access to divine consciousness. This part of the mind is mostly undiscovered and underdeveloped in most of humanity.

Dolores created a unique method of hypnosis, Quantum Healing Hypnosis Technique (QHHT), that opened a doorway to the client's subconscious mind to explore other lifetimes and realms in Creation. When I use the word "quantum," I am speaking to the fabric of Consciousness, the multidimensional unified field of Creation. When clients are in these hypnotic states, they tap into the part of their consciousness that is nonlocal and connected to All That Is. This includes access to other lifetimes, other realities and dimensions, and other intelligent consciousness forms (i.e., higher-dimensional light beings, telepathic extraterrestrials, etc.). Through this experience, clients came to understand another perspective and origin of self-sabotaging and limiting beliefs that were playing out in this life and the core mental/emotional patterns that create illness and disease.

During her sessions, Dolores started to contact a part of her clients' consciousness that seemed to have endless knowledge and wisdom. She called this aspect of her clients the Subconscious or the SC. Others have called this the Higher Self, the oversoul, superconsciousness, or the cosmic consciousness. I prefer the term Higher Self and superconscious mind and go into great detail of how to activate and evolve superconsciousness throughout this text. While the information was limitless, the SC/Higher Self would only answer questions in a way that was appropriate for the client's learning path and honored their free will. When working with the SC, both Dolores and the client described powerful healing energy in their bodies and the treatment room. Clients often reported instantaneous healing as they were transformed from the inside out during the session. While this may seem too good to be true, there are countless documented and measurable occurrences where clients received lasting miraculous healing through these types of sessions.

When she would work with the Higher Self, this higher consciousness identity and supportive Light team would speak through the client as a collective consciousness as if the client were speaking in third-person perspective about themselves. "We are always guiding her. We wish she would follow her intuition more." and "We are beginning to use white light to heal this now." are common examples of how "They" (i.e., SC/Higher Self) express themselves and heal the client during the session.

The healing work is always done with unconditional love and honors the free will and sovereignty of the client. If instantaneous healing was not "appropriate" for the client's growth and spiritual maturation, "They" would suggest what steps the client should take to heal themselves. Slowly, over many years, Dolores's work expanded as "They" introduced more components to the healing process so that she could evolve her work and teach it to others.

The Three Waves of Volunteers and the New Earth was one of nineteen books written by Dolores Cannon before her transition out of physical life. Each book contains transcriptions of client sessions describing detailed events from other lives while using her Quantum Healing Hypnosis Technique (QHHT).

Awakening to the Starseed Volunteer Mission

After several years of working with clients worldwide, Dolores noticed a pattern of clients describing a massive galactic and higher dimensional mission to raise the vibration of the planet and shift it into a new reality called the New Earth. The book describes how countless numbers of advanced spiritual beings from distant star systems, and even other universes, volunteered to incarnate on the Earth with a mission to raise consciousness on the planet and assist with this grand transition.

The New Earth is a higher frequency Earth reality that exists in a higher dimension than we are in now. Clients describe a large-scale plan initiated by Source Intelligence (God) to reset life on planet Earth back to the original template of a harmonic environment thriving within diversity. Parallel to this, Dolores's work described a shift in human consciousness from a duality-based mindset to a heart-centered, multidimensional consciousness and a less physical body of light.

The First Wave Volunteers were born beginning around 1945 through the 1970s. They were like a stealthy reconnaissance mission. First on the scene. First to patrol and feel out the collective consciousness vibrations. First to introduce the higher consciousness perspectives to the masses. Many had a difficult and lonely time since there were not many other humans in higher, love-based spiritual consciousness on the planet at the time.

The Second Wave Volunteers were born around the late 1970s through

1990s and are channels for higher spiritual energy and divine wisdom. These souls came in with a higher level of intuitive gifts and are often extremely sensitive to energy. Many are hands-on healers, musicians, vocalists, yoga teachers, and so on. They are space-holders who transmit a new frequency out to the field of Earth, bridging the old ways with the new ways and consciousness of New Earth.

The Third Wave Volunteers, the younger generations, are builders and innovative geniuses in science, spirituality, technology, and so on. They are divinely inspired visionaries that will build the New Earth. They are radical lovers and shine bright with crystalline eyes and have achieved high consciousness levels in other lifetimes. Some of these souls have never had a physical incarnation or have come straight from Source as new souls with pure Light and no karma.

I have been told all the children born at this time are part of this Grand Mission. They are pure souls, evolutionary masters, here to build the New Earth. More is written about the Starseed Mission and phenomena later in this book.

As I was reading Dolores's book, I felt I was reading my own story. I felt the truth in her words. Suddenly so many things made sense about my life. I finally had answers to why I felt so different from others in my community and family. I understood why I felt other people's emotions and could tell what people were thinking. It all started to click together. I was so excited to share the book with Ron, my husband and co-founder of New Earth Ascending, who also deeply resonated with the material.

At the same time, we were beginning to work with an Australian musical group as dancers for their "Return of the Bird Tribes" tour for their album by the same name. Something about the term "bird tribes" caught my attention, and I started to research it. I found the book by the same name, written by Ken Carey, in 1988 that describes a prophecy of high spiritual beings returning to the Earth at a time of spiritual renewal.

Many cultures describe times when culture-bringing beings would come from the heavens or from across the waters to bring technology and information to humanity throughout history. Thoth went to the Egyptians, White Buffalo Calf Woman went to the Native Americans, Quetzalcoatl went to the Aztecs, the Seven Sisters of the Pleiades went to the Aboriginal people of Australia, beings from the Sirius A and B binary star system went to the Dogon people of Mali; and many other stories exist in many other cultures. Carey's book described when these beings would come again during a time of spiritual awakening on the planet.

I was receiving information from multiple directions and was going through a massive realignment with my soul's purpose as I became aware of this greater story and mission. Ron and I went to an arts festival in the desert of Nevada called Burning Man. While we were there, a couple excitedly recognized us as "twin flames" and asked us which star system we had come from. "We are from Sirius. Where are you from? Orion? The Pleiades? Sirius?" she asked. The concept of "starseeds" and "twin flames" was new to me, and I did not know what to say. I saw a special sparkle in the couple's eyes and felt that I should do some research to understand more about it.

After some research and some magical synchronicities, Ron convinced me that we should do the QHHT training and certification process. I was super resistant to learning it because of deep religious programming and egoic structures that made me doubtful of the truthfulness of the work. I was familiar with reincarnation but did not necessarily believe in it. Eventually, I gave in to Ron's suggestion and took the QHHT course.

Evolving Beyond QHHT

In the early stages of practicing QHHT, Ron and I were guided to start doing the sessions online to share the technique's power with as many people as we could. This method was not permitted by the organization because Dolores did not believe it to be safe and her organization does not permit it still. Dolores was an elder and this type of technology was new to her, whereas the younger generations are much more comfortable interfacing with video conferencing.

We have been told by the Higher Consciousness that there is nothing to fear, and NOW is the time to spread these healing methods across the world in whatever way is possible. To honor our lineage and teacher, we stopped using the name QHHT and started experimenting with different names as our way of practicing quantum healing evolved beyond our initial training.

Online sessions are just as powerful as in-person sessions and are often more comfortable and affordable for the client. It is completely safe to facilitate sessions remotely, and we have had countless powerful sessions that have been facilitated in this way. Dolores's organization does not allow adaptation of the QHHT technique. Its practitioners need to perform the method exactly how Dolores taught and not add any modifications or outside techniques. While it is important to protect the work's integrity, this rigidity does not permit the work to expand to its full potential. We are in a time of expansion and evolution, and we must always be open to the transformation and progression of all methods we currently use or risk leaving them in the past as everything on the Earth is evolving.

Another topic that caused us to evolve beyond our initial training of QHHT was the organization's strict denial of negative spiritual attachment and what felt like shaming those who believed in this common experience. Ron and I and other quantum healing practitioners discovered that certain psychological, emotional, and physical imbalances were being created by pervasive energies that did not belong to the client's energy field that had somehow become attached to the client. This includes spirit attachments, curses from past lives, and implants from nefarious beings to name a few. QHHT did not provide us with appropriate training to work with these serious complications. If it were found out that a practitioner had adopted these practices and still operated under the name of QHHT, practitioners could be removed from the QHHT directory.

Many practitioners have reported spontaneous visitation from Dolores through clients under hypnosis where she has encouraged practitioners to follow their intuitive guidance and continue to develop the work through experimentation just as she did when she developed QHHT.

We were inspired greatly by other quantum healing practitioners' extraction methods and crafted our own approaches to clearing pervasive energies and spirit attachments. The reality of negative thought-forms, negative extraterrestrial implants, and entity attachment is too big to ignore, considering so many cases are emerging, not to forget the thousands of years of wisdom and extraction practices passed down by Indigenous peoples and various wisdom traditions.

We never assume that someone has an entity just because they suffer, and we do not bring it up in our intake interview. Once the client is deep in a hypnotic trance, we ask the Higher Self if there are entities or attached energies. If the answer is yes, then we ask questions to understand how this occurred and if the client has anything to learn to release negative attachment. From there, the Higher Self can immediately extract the energy and take it back into the Light for healing. It is all extremely safe, insightful, and benefits all who are involved. We have found that, often, the revelation of spirit attachment or implants will not occur unless the practitioner asks and gives permission for a scan specifically for attached energies. Ron and I believe this is because of the honoring of the free will of the entities involved in the experience of attachment.

In my opinion, to continue to deny such experiences is a disservice to the clients who come to us seeking answers and healing. All practices and traditions can become dogmatic if we do not allow the evolution of thought to take us into new frontiers of consciousness. These are evolutionary practices, and we need to be constantly open to shifting our paradigm so that we can offer the best guidance and support with the changing of times.

Once we started offering quantum healing sessions online, clients started coming to Ron and me from all over the world. Not only were the sessions powerfully healing and transformative for the clients, but we were also going through a rapid transformation as we learned about ancient stories and galactic events from the perspective of souls embodied at those times. While Dolores taught that many people had "potato-picking lives," simple lives with simple themes, it seemed that almost every session of mine had to do with the New Earth Mission, powerful events from the ancient past, and future timelines of Earth.

I soon realized that I was getting a theme and timeline in my sessions. The timeline given to me via my clients describes how Creation came into being, ancient galactic history, the seeding of life on Earth, the rise and fall of ancient civilizations, the true teachings of Jesus through the eyes of people that were closest to him, information about the transformation of the human body to a less dense body of Light, and the evolution of the Earth into the higher frequency reality of New Earth. In less than a year, I went from a reincarnation skeptic to believing that anything is possible, and that the multiverse is more incredible than we can even imagine!

Illuminated Quantum Healing

After years of practicing and evolving how we do this work, Ron and I have created our own quantum healing method that incorporates all that we have learned on our path. This includes facilitating sessions online to reach as many people as possible to assist in this Great Awakening.

Our training method acknowledges spirit attachment and teaches our facilitators how to perform negative spirit releasement. We teach yogic psychology, holistic wellness concepts, and energy healing methods to ensure the practitioner has a thorough understanding of human consciousness and how to lead the client through the ascension process using multiple IQH sessions and mentorship programs. We call our method Illuminated Quantum Healing. IQH can be learned in live classes or through our online course offered on our social network Source⊙Energy.

Illuminated Quantum Healing (IQH) is a personal transformation method for multidimensional holistic healing and consciousness development. IQH incorporates energy healing, meditative practices, yogic philosophy, and hypnosis skills to reconcile limiting subconscious patterning and integrate instantaneous multidimensional healing and wisdom from one's Higher Self.

I am deeply honored to be a part of this work. I am so blessed to have an opportunity to work with such incredible people and energies. Each session that I facilitate nourishes me to the core, and I have the sublime opportunity to observe miraculous instantaneous healing and transformation in my clients. After witnessing the infinite potential of quantum healing hypnosis, I firmly believe that we can ascend beyond all states of illness and disease and that we have infinite support to move beyond the shadows of our past and become a new People of Light.

Getting to the New Earth involves a process of spiritual growth and purification. To transition with the Earth, it is required that we raise our vibration to match the accelerating frequency of the Earth as it changes. Mostly, this is about releasing fear and negative karma. I have written this book as a tool to use for your spiritual awakening and transformation that many are calling Ascension. This is my gift to humanity to help make the process easier and explain different components to cultivate a deeper understanding of this Grand Shift to New Earth and our newly evolving Lightbody.

Spiritual awakening and ascension are available for ALL people no matter what they have done in their past, current economic status, gender expression, sexuality, religion, etc. There are as many paths to the New Earth as there are humans on the planet. No one religion holds the keys or the way to heaven. The power is within YOU!

To support the global ascension process, we have created New Earth Ascending. New Earth Ascending is a non-profit, faith-based organization focused on global ascension and establishing heart-centered, sustainable communities and educational centers around the world.

Alongside Illuminated Quantum Healing (IQH), Ron and I have created other pathways of support for the global ascension process:

1. Embodied Light Reiki Training and Certification
2. New Earth Ascending has three levels of Reiki certification to train people how to channel divine light for healing. These trainings honor the lineage and teachings of the Usui System of Natural Healing while also infusing evolutionary concepts and practices that go beyond standard Reiki training.
3. Online courses for awakening and ascension are available on our private social network Source⊙Energy. The courses include philosophical exploration on several models of spiritual growth and alchemical practices to support your healing, awakening, and ascension. These courses include meditations, holistic wellness education, breathwork, lightbody activation and more. These courses lay foundational understanding for beginners and move through a progression of intermediate and advanced practices and knowledge.
4. TransformOtion was created to support the embodiment of one's Higher Self using dance, somatic movement, yogic practices, meditation, imagination, and energy healing. This fusion of practices helps to purify and repair the physical, etheric, and mental bodies so that one can move beyond perceived limitations into boundless rhythm and flow. Through this interweaving of multiple disciplinary paths, we integrate physicality with transcendental ecstatic play while cultivating a deep connection with and trust in the body's wisdom.

    These ideas and concepts can be used for personal embodiment and activation or infused into performance art to create powerful alchemical experiences for the performer and the audience. This fusion of high art and spiritual transformation creates a multidimensional experience for all who are within the field of performance energies.

5. Source⊙Energy is a social network exclusively for those on the path of ascension to connect and share inspiration as we manifest and build a New Earth. We invite all souls who feel aligned with New Earth to join this network and add your unique energy and love to this community. Source⊙Energy serves as a pathway of social interaction and is the home of our online courses and training.
6. Children are our future. Youth inspiration and enrichment programming is in development to assist the spiritual activation and consciousness mastery of the youth. NEA is dedicated to creating harmonic environments and rich educational programs to guide youth to connect with cosmic intelligence and embody their divine nature and mastery as they build the New Earth.

Ron and I have dedicated our lives to supporting this Grand Transition. We stand alongside all of you as humanity awakens to its True Nature and becomes a People of Light in the heavenly reality of New Earth.

New Earth Ascending is dedicated to assisting people to realize their divinity and manifest that truth in every aspect of their life. For more information about New Earth Ascending or to contact Michael, please scan the QR code below for a list of resources and links, or visit *www.newearthascending.org*. Be sure to check out our courses including the Illuminated Quantum Healing practitioner course.

New Earth Ascending is a registered 508 (c)(1)(a) Self-Supported Non-profit Church Ministry with a global outreach. We greatly appreciate your support as we create new systems, communities, and schools for the development of the New Earth civilization. If you would like to make a tax-deductible donation to support our mission, please go to:

https://donorbox.org/donationtonewearthascending

Scan with a smart device camera for more information!

NEW EARTH ASCENDING VISIONARY CREED

We acknowledge the sovereignty and equality of all levels of Creation and support the liberation of all of Life from cycles of suffering. We believe in the power of divine sovereign creatorship endowed to us by God/Source and dedicate our life to Light and Love in service to All. We believe in conscious participation, empowering everyone to activate awakening in themselves and their community.

We recognize free will and surrender our will and desires to the higher will of the Divine. We believe in divine timing and practice trust, patience, and tolerance as we witness the unfoldment of the perfection of the Divine Plan. We believe in the potency of empowering prayer, meditation, and ritual as tools for communication with the Divine for the culmination of spiritual light and divine wisdom. We believe everyone has a direct connection to the Source and no intermediary is needed. When we come together in fellowship, prayer, and devotion, we amplify the light of each individuals' loving intention through our unified, heart-centered consciousness.

We seek to uplift all groups and communities so that we may celebrate our unity, diversity, and wholeness. New Earth Ascending is non-competitive and embraces an ecumenical relationship with all religions and wisdom traditions. We believe in interfaith and inter-spirituality, acknowledging the teachings of Light, Love, and Wisdom in many traditions, philosophies, and cultures. We believe that no single religion holds the keys to the Kingdom of God and the blessings of redemption are available to all people through their unbreakable innate connection to the Godhead.

We believe in the Law of Oneness and that all of Creation emanates from one Divine Source that has both masculine and feminine principles. As we heal and balance the divine masculine and divine feminine principles within us, we embody the divine androgyny of Source and Nature as a harmonic synthesis of Spirit and Matter.

We believe that humanity and planet Earth are going through a rapid physical and spiritual transformation called by many as The Ascension or The Event. We believe this process to be part of a higher evolutionary divine plan guided by the Source of Creation and legions of beings working for the Light. This evolutionary process is multidimensional and is beyond the standard biological evolution spoken of by modern science.

We believe that we, as humanity, are awakening to our spiritual Self and are becoming a heart-based, unity-focused species with higher, multidimensional awareness, which some call Christ Consciousness, Cosmic Consciousness, or 5D Consciousness. We believe this transformation's power is happening through our divinely designed and curated DNA as the physical body transforms into a less dense body of Light with tremendously expanded multidimensional abilities.

We believe that Planet Earth, the sentient being of Gaia, is going through a similar restoration process and will soon transform into a revitalized higher dimensional planet, which many are calling the New Earth. Earth changes, weather events, crumbling institutional structures, frequency fluctuations, and astrological phenomena are all signs that we are nearing that shift into the next Golden Age, where Heaven and Earth become one and all systems of control and limitation will fall away.

We believe that we are supported by benevolent higher dimensional, subterranean, and extraterrestrial beings that work in harmonic collaboration with the higher evolutionary Divine Plan of Source. We believe that soon humanity will be consciously reunited with these benevolent beings and serve the higher evolutionary plan of the Light and Love of Source as cosmic co-citizens of the Multiverse working as one Family of Light in service to all of Creation.

We understand that the pathway of Self/Source-Realization and Ascension is comprised of self-study, self-practice, self-discipline, and steadfastness. We practice self-care and self-purification to clarify our Light. We acknowledge and value the acceleration of this process when we practice together in groupings of two or more in fellowship and worship.

We strive to grow in awareness and focused attention, practicing mindfulness in all areas of our lives to grow as conscious, heart-centered creators. We choose to focus our life positively with faith and knowing that Life is evolving in perfection following the Divine Plan of the Supreme Source.

We believe in the power of intention. We practice nonviolence and non-harmfulness in intention, thought, and action. We strive to release all forms of judgment and dual thinking. We honor the sacred heart's radiant potential and believe loving compassion and understanding to be The Way. We practice the heart-centered qualities of gentleness, reverence, loving-kindness, and forgiveness as pathways to reconciliation to emulate the eternal grace of Source and our Earth Mother, Gaia.

We see that Truth is alive within each of us, and we practice inner reflection to grow in discernment for what energies are resonant with our inner Source and our path. We practice benevolent truthfulness, honesty, straightforwardness, and vulnerability to embody and vocalize our deepest truth.

We value and practice transparency and accountability, believing in the opportunity for spiritual growth through spiritual partnership with our community members. We recognize one another as divine mirrors, reflecting to us where we are in our vibration, beliefs, and intentions.

We practice sacred sexuality as an alchemical tool for Divine Union and Ascension. We strive to purify our intentions and desires to align with Higher Love and authentic connection. We believe in heart-based self and consensual mutual pleasure to unite body, mind, and spirit so that we may deepen in our love and authentic connection to our Divine Self, our partner(s), and Creation.

We practice contentment, acceptance, appreciation, and gratitude for our life's many blessings and lessons. We practice non-attachment, non-possessiveness, non-stealing, non-excess, and sustainability, for all we need is given to us through our alignment with our Creator Source and our connection to our Earth Mother. We practice stewardship and sustainable selfless service, acknowledging our responsibility to take care of the world around us and within.

We practice sacred commerce, investing our resources, time, and energy towards the greater good and sustainability of our community and planet. We believe in reciprocal energy exchange and strive to do so when able. We practice generosity, hospitality, and charitability as reflections of the abundance of the Universe.

We strive to embody and emulate these spiritual principles to manifest the complete liberation of all beings from cycles of suffering and to assist this Grand Transition into the New Earth.

Bless us all!

GATEWAY ONE: ASCENSION INITIATION

Keys for Higher Evolution

This section describes the higher evolutionary pathway of the transmigrating soul and the purpose of incarnation and Ascension. It also includes a presentation and exploration of Universal Law and a description of the progression of consciousness through cosmic evolutionary cycles.

ONE

The Shift of the Ages

Humanity stands at the brink of unprecedented transformation, a gigantic quantum leap in consciousness that has been foretold by many prophets in many cultures throughout history. This is the Omega phase, the ending of a grand experimental cycle where all the karma of Earth and humanity will be reconciled as the Earth is transformed into a higher light spectrum reality commonly known as the New Earth. In unison, humanity is going through its own transformation process to become a civilization of Light, divine beings in sophisticated bodies of Light who operate from a liberated and expanded multidimensional consciousness.

Ascension was brought into the collective consciousness of humanity through the teachings of Christ Jesus, also known as Yeshua ben Joseph, the Master of Light for Planet Earth. This rapid transformation process is supported by leagues of benevolent extraterrestrial and ultraterrestrial beings that form a Hierarchy of Light that serves a higher evolution following a Divine Plan established by the Source of Creation. As humanity and Earth ascends, we will be consciously reunited with the Hierarchy of Light and the Star Nations and live as cooperative cosmic citizens united in a higher consciousness reality.

In my attempt to describe the indescribable, I will mostly refer to the Supreme Consciousness and all its functions as the Source of Creation or simply Source. For me, this term accurately describes what many commonly call God. Some traditions have different names for Source in pre-manifestation such as *Ein Soph* or *Brahman* and another term for God with manifested attributes like *Ein Soph Or*, *Ishvara*, or *Logos*. For simplicity, I will simply use the term Source to speak for both the transcendental and manifested expressions of the Supreme Consciousness. Many people have turned their backs on the Divine and religious institutions because of the pain and suffering created by dogma, sexual abuse, hypocrisy, religious wars, and oppression. Each person carries a unique definition and set of internal images and emotions evoked by the word "God." While some people believe in a higher power of some kind, others reject the idea of a god-man in the clouds punishing and judging the world for their sins. Some can at least recognize some type of higher connection to nature. Some have decided to have nothing to do with spirituality and the divine and choose to stick with modern versions of science and what they can sense through their five senses.

The dualistic philosophy of Samkhya speaks of Source in terms of *Purusha* and *Prakriti*. *Purusha* is the pure consciousness, the Seer of Creation. *Purusha* in the human is the Self, the *Atman*, the pure Source within that observes this bodymind and this universe. *Prakriti*, Sanskrit for Nature or Creation, is everything in manifestation, everything with a name and form. This includes all universes, all dimensions and realities including the higher "heavenly" light dimensions, and our concept of God.

Prakriti can also be called *maya*, a Sanskrit term commonly translated as illusion or magic. Source through its power of *maya* projects this entire universe including the bodymind complex you find yourself in. When people say only Source is real and everything else is false, an illusion, it is because all names and forms borrow existence from the Eternal Source, the Pure Consciousness that you truly are.

Maya not only projects names and forms into creation but it also veils the True Reality. A classic example of the power of *maya* is when a person sees a rope out of the corner of their eye and mistakenly thinks it is a snake. *Maya* has veiled the true nature of the rope, so one sees a snake. At the most fundamental level, the Absolute level, neither the snake no the rope exists. It is Source using its power of maya to project a whole reality which includes the rope which one confuses as a snake, a dream within a dream, within a dream.

Another classic example of this is water which comes in many names and forms. Whether we call it an ocean, a glacier, fog, or mist it is all water. All these objects with different names and forms borrow existence from the water. In the same way, all is Source appearing as universes, planets, individual plants, animals, good people, evil people, energy, and emotion. Yet all of it borrows existence from Source, the pure Consciousness which you are.

One of the purposes of *Prakriti*, of *maya*, is to test the Seer's ability to perceive the True Source that is behind all manifestations. *Maya* arises, abides, and dissolves in an ever-changing landscape pulling our senses and awareness in every direction. *Maya* seduces us and ensnares our consciousness in the pull of sensory experiences and deepens our misidentification with our bodymind, distracting our attention from our True Nature. We falsely believe that all we see, touch, taste, smell, feel, and think is real and become enamored by the dream of reality, overlooking our True Nature. It is a game we play with our Oneself. A game of forgetting and remembering who we truly are as Pure Consciousness.

Our perceived reality is like a distorted funhouse mirror that bends, shrinks, and accentuates the reflected image. The thing with a funhouse mirror is that most people can keep the awareness that what they are seeing is not real. In a physical body, it is much harder to stay aware that only Source is the true reality and that all the rest is smoke and mirrors. It is our own complex inner reality that is projected and outpictured, distorting and hypnotizing our mind into emotional intoxication and spiritual amnesia.

In physical life, the initiate is tested in their ability to stay laser-focused on the true reality of Divine Love in the background of all experiences and to invite what is normally in the background of experience into the foreground so that the "face of God" is all that one perceives.

Sometimes in my hypnosis sessions, a client returns to the Source. Typically, they describe the environment as being a bright warm light and that they feel so loved. They say that many other beings are there and that everything feels so good there. Sometimes they say something like, "We are many, but we are all one." I ask them how long they have been there, and they often respond with something like "There is no time here." or "What do you mean? We have always been here." I usually let the client experience this for a few minutes to deeply remember the love they came from and truly are. Often clients are crying tears of joy as years of trauma and struggle begin to melt away through the power of union with Source. It is a powerful and beautiful thing to witness.

Interfaith dialogue recognizes the threads of harmonic commonality found in religious and spiritual texts, philosophy, humanitarian beliefs, and science. As humanity awakens, many realize that there is a common foundation in all these traditions and viewpoints of what "God" is and the meaning of Life.

As we move forward on the New Earth timeline, we can release our wounds from religious dogma and be open to the teachings of Light and

Unconditional Love inherently found within the sacred texts from ancient cultures and world traditions. We can drop the dogma of dead religions focused on fear and condemnation and find the indwelling of the Living Source Within and claim our divine inheritance.

When I speak of Creation, I am speaking of the holographic Multiverse. The Multiverse has been described by several different mystical philosophies and esoteric wisdom traditions using different terms to describe the various planes and subplanes of reality. They all seem to agree on one plane that is the substratum of all the other planes, the plane of the Absolute, Source, or God. From this Absolute Reality all other planes and subplanes emerge. Another level of reality is the Transactional Reality of Relativity, the realm of phenomenon where the Light of Consciousness interacts in different forms with varying frequencies and polarizations interacting in varying planes of light density. This level would include the physical plane we are in and the higher experimental light dimensions. Another level is the Reality of Illusion such as mirages or the reality we experience in our dream states which appears real until we are in our waking consciousness.

Just like in lucid dreaming where the Dreamer awakens in the dream, another level of awakening can happen during our waking consciousness. When the soul is ready, spiritual consciousness begins to stir awake and higher knowledge leads their consciousness out of entanglement with the Transactional Reality towards the realization of the Ultimate Reality which is both imminent and transcendent. God-Source is both beyond the knowable universe and the Universal Principle which pervades all realities, realms, planes, and dimensions. This is what Christ meant when he said to go within to find the Kingdom of God. All that you seek is already within, yet you must seek it to find it.

All of Creation exists within a continuum of ascending and descending movement patterning to and from the Source. Divine Light flows from this Source out into many levels and layers of Creation, universes within universes, existing in various states of light density. Within these multidimensional experimental zones of Light exist a multitude of species, physical and nonphysical, in various states of evolution with each plane of Creation working in symbiotic relationship within a unified field of Source Consciousness. As the light descends in frequency, we arrive at the physical dimension, the material plane that our universe exists in. Light descends from the higher dimensions and is projected through one Great Central Sun of this universe which pulses evolutionary coding through a vast stellar "modem" network of fixed stars. Each Central Sun broadcasts multidimensional light coding to evolve each "theater" of evolution" in accordance with the higher plan of the Divine.

Eventually, we arrive at our Sun, the central star of our solar system, which emanates all the intelligent coding for the evolution of countless levels of life forms and celestial bodies in our solar system. Even each planet in our solar system is connected through a web of subtle energy pathways that support the other celestial bodies. Everything, including each individual human, is connected within this web of evolutionary communication and complex multidimensional configuration.

At the beginning of Creation, the Divine Intelligence sent out parts of its Oneself to create, learn, and explore. When I use the word "soul," I am speaking of the individual lightbody essence, the conglomerate of subtle bodies, that has been sent into the realms of Creation to learn and create with free will. This part takes on lessons and karma as a way of learning and growing as it ascends back towards the realization of its true origin and true nature which I refer to as the Source within, the Atman, the Witness, or pure Consciousness.

The soul is immortal, has lived many incarnations, and will release the physical body upon its death experience and continue its evolutionary journey in other forms. The soul is a portion of what I call the oversoul, which is a higher density form of your consciousness that exists beyond this physical dimension of reality which you will be consciously reconnected with as we shift into the fifth dimensional (5D) also called 4th Density, New Earth reality. The oversoul is like a quantum information storehouse of all the information collected from all of its many soul aspects which have lived myriad lifetimes throughout eternity.

The Hindu traditions describe the journey of ascension as *jiva* (personal self) as it awakens to Atman (Source within) or Brahman (God/Source), experienced as Eternal Existence, Eternal Consciousness, and Eternal Bliss. The Kabbalistic/Jewish traditions describe it at the journey of the *Nephesh* (soul) that is matured into *Neshamah* (sovereign soul or Spirit-soul Synthesis) through the ministering Spirit (*Ruach*). The Buddhists describe it as an awakening to the Buddha within. The Hare Krishnas describe it as the path to Krishnahood or Krishna Consciousness. The Christians call it being "saved" and following the path of Christ. The New Age community calls it ascending to Christ Consciousness. Each of these beautiful traditions and philosophies describes the same ascension process and the same spark of the Creator within all of us that has taken on karma to learn and grow through a process of God-Realization.

While there may be differences in practices or conflicting philosophies in some of these traditions, there is a beautiful interweaving of them all that can give us keys and insight into the greater tapestry of Creation. There are infinite philosophies, infinite practices of devotion, and infinite pathways of Ascension back to the Source. All of these wisdom traditions lead to the same Source, the same Love, the same Light. If you are reading this text, you can rest assured that you are on your unique path of Ascension.

Throughout this book, I will speak of intention and consciousness in terms of service-to-self negative polarity (STS), and service-to-all (STA), positive polarity, which some call service-to-others (STO). Religions speak of "good" and "evil" with a charge of judgment. The problem is everyone has a different definition of what those terms mean.

Service-to-self (STS) consciousness is when we serve our false self, our ego, often at the expense of others. The negative polarity in our consciousness is all about me, me, me! Individuals in the negative polarity are concerned with self-preservation and the accumulation of external power. Negatively polarized consciousness manifests as passive aggression, selfishness, greed, pride, domination, control, egoism, and so on. Individuals and groups that are negatively polarized are often also called "dark," "evil," or tyrannical as the fullest expression of negative polarity is consciousness cemented fully in material reality and is void of higher spiritual intelligence and empathy.

Service-to-all (STA) consciousness is a mindset of honoring and protecting the expansion, freedom, and joy of the world around you while respecting your own inner being, sovereignty, and alignment. Positively polarized consciousness manifests as gentleness, benevolent truth speaking, healthy boundaries, forgiveness, devotion, and all other attitudes and actions of harmony and stewardship. People holding a high level of positive polarity consistently act altruistically and from a place of loving compassion and spiritual unity. Individuals and groups from the positive polarity are often called "good," "holy," and "light," as they reflect the benevolence and goodness of the Divine.

This concept speaks to something deeper than action and points to the underlying intention that drives thought, speech, and action. Someone may appear to be positively polarized, service-to-all, but in actuality is using nicety to manipulate others or protect their ego-self. Conversely, someone may be judged as "negative" because they say something that stirs up chaos but, in actuality, are doing so because of their commitment to truth and goodness. Look at what happened to Jesus. Even as "the world" projected hatred and judgment on him, his actions were for goodwill.

We all hold consciousness that is of both sides of polarity. As we begin to awaken, we begin to transform our negative polarity into positive polarity by aligning with our deepest truth and the unity of the compassionate heart. We move from an STS, negatively polarized, expression into an STA, positively polarized embodiment of righteousness, unconditional love, and spiritual sovereignty.

Earth has been an experimental zone for the full spectrum of thought, from the evilest and most negatively polarized to the most sublime and pure expressions of consciousness. That experiment is ending as the negative polarity, the service-to-self consciousness thought-forms, will no longer be permitted in the New Earth reality. So now we see all of those ways we have hidden from our True Nature coming to the surface to be reconciled by compassion and noble action. Those shifting to the 5D New Earth consciousness are those who are making the polarity switch and raising their overall vibration. Truly, unconditional love and unity consciousness is the way to the New Earth.

The Event

For some time now, highly charged photonic waves have been broadcasting from the Great Central Sun of our universe, pulsating from central sun to central sun carrying streams of divinely encoded evolutionary energies that are revitalizing and renewing all that they touch. These Light information pulsations are awakening the consciousness of humanity from the duality of polarized consciousness towards the awakened and liberated higher consciousness that many are calling christ consciousness, cosmic consciousness, or oversoul consciousness. Christ consciousness is not only for those of a mainstream religion. This consciousness is available to all people who choose to live a life of unconditional love and unity. It is the pure Light consciousness of the Universe, and it is your birthright to realize this capacity in yourself as a liberated being of Light.

Space Weather and the Schumann Resonance

Some of these evolutionary energy events are being picked up with modern technology. Solar events like solar wind, coronal mass ejections, and solar flares bring major upgrades to the planet. I have noticed that when the solar wind reaches 400 km/sec, I start having headaches, chest tension, dehydration, and emotional sensitivity. The higher the solar wind speed, the more amplified these symptoms are. When solar wind speed reaches 600 km/sec or higher, I am either wiped out, emotional, need lots of water, or I feel like I am riding a wave of bliss and insight. Everyone handles these energy waves differently and there are simple self-care practices and protocols that you can implement to help the integration process. These are mentioned later in the book.

Another measurement to watch is the Schumann Resonance. The Schumann Resonance measures Earth's atmosphere's electromagnetic frequencies found in the cavity between Earth's surface and the ionosphere. The lowest frequency mode and fundamental Schumann Resonance is 7.83 Hz, followed by harmonics of 14 Hz, 20 Hz, 26 Hz, 33 Hz, 39 Hz, and 45 Hz (rounded numbers for the sake of simplicity). It has been found that when the wave size or amplitude of these frequencies increases, we may experience direct effects on our electromagnetic fields causing fluctuations in our emotions, cognition, cardiac system, and consciousness. I have been following an online Schumann Resonance monitor associated with the Tomsk State University in Tomsk, Russia for the last few years. I have noticed a direct relationship between fluctuations of the Earth's frequencies and my own mental, emotional, etheric, and physical experiences that I call ascension symptoms.

It should be noted that sensitive people worldwide also report "ascension symptoms" even when the measurable frequencies (space weather and Schumann) are not present. I believe that these energies are coming from a source that humanity does not have measurement technologies for at the time. This can include friendly spacecraft, distant planets and stars, and other sources, including the Photon Belt. Earth will be passing through the Photon Belt for around another 2,000 years, which will dramatically accelerate the ascension processes. These light waves are building in intensity and potency gradually changing all of life as we know it on the planet.

We cannot even imagine the world we are about to awaken to from our current consciousness level. Each wave awakens another group of souls on the New Earth trajectory and begins their healing, activation, and divine embodiment process. Those who have awakened before the rest of humanity will experience "The Event" as a series of waves and upgrading energies that gradually lead us into higher and higher consciousness. For others, they will continue in the lower dimensional consciousness until they experience a wave that awakens them to their higher consciousness as the planet makes its ascension into the New Earth reality. All of this was designed pre-incarnation and we are watching the timings play out.

There are many people who build up a lot of emotion expecting a major solar event that instantly awakens and changes the Earth. This may or may not happen as the many timelines and probabilities play out. In some ways, the Solar Flash has become a "savior program" for many. In truth, all experiences arise within the Light of our own Self. We are the Solar Flash! We are the Divine Plan in action!

After these energy waves leave the Sun, they make contact with the biofield/aura of Earth. After the energy passes through the Earth's electromagnetic fields, the energies enter our biofield and begin to enter the tissues and cells of our body. These energies carry intelligent coding that is evolving every cell of our body to a less dense bioluminous body of light. Human DNA is evolving beyond the typical two strands to a fully activated and revitalized 12-strand system. We are returning to our "Adamic" form, the original divine human blueprint.

Each energy wave brings in new ascension symptoms as the whole human body and consciousness system is upgraded. Every individual is unique in this experience. Many report headaches, cold-like symptoms, hot flashes, ringing in the ears, vivid dreams, burning in the chest, digestive system issues, detoxification symptoms, emotional purging, and more. I talk more about these symptoms and ascension symptom care later in the book.

It should be noted that not all of humanity will be making this transition. These plans were made before incarnating and are not the polarized judgment narrative propagated by world religions. This is part of the Divine Plan, and all souls are playing a part in the great story that is unfolding. Those who will not be transitioning will not be receiving the upgrades to their genetics and will start to deteriorate in health and transition out of the body.

There is nothing "bad" about this. They have simply fulfilled their life plans and will transition out of the body to support the ascension from the spirit side and/or prepare to incarnate again in another form, either on Earth or another planet/realm where they can continue their soul's evolutionary pathway. Physical death is not final. We are immortal beings who have lived many times and will continue to evolve and serve Creation through many more forms in the future.

The Unveiling

Apocalypse is a Greek word meaning "unveiling," "uncovering," or "revelation." This implies that what was once hidden is to be brought into the light of awareness. We see this in the unfolding of events around the world as the unconscious shadow is being brought to the surface to be cleared. In the coming months, we will see more political scandals surfacing and the unveiling of travesties that have been committed over time and kept hidden from the public.

Turn off the Television: Tune into Your Inner Being

Repeatedly in my hypnosis sessions, it has been suggested to turn off the news stations, put down the smartphones, and tune into the presence of Gaia, the Divine Source, and our own Inner Being. The gateway to this new Light Kingdom (Queendom if you prefer) of New Earth is through the electromagnetic field of your own heart and your innate connection to the Grace and Light of Source. Ascension requires us to grow in our capacity to love unconditionally and transform our physical, etheric, and mental bodies through transformative practices and purification. This is what Christ meant when he said to "clean thy robes" to prepare for the next "garment of Light."

This book serves as a guide to illuminate the Ascension pathway and initiate the reader to the Higher Mysteries and Laws of Creation. It aims to explain our origins from the eternal Source and provides a summary of the story of Creation as it relates to cosmic, galactic, planetary, and human history. It gives a futuristic perspective of the revitalized higher dimensional Earth post-Ascension that describes what the New Earth will be like and how humanity will live upon the Earth and with the Star Nations and Hierarchy of Light.

There is a detailed description of the stages of Ascension as it relates to the evolution of the planet, human biology, and human consciousness.

The reader's consciousness is guided into an experiential relationship with their Lightbody, and spiritual energy practices are given to activate, heal, and upgrade the human subtle energy body in preparation for the next "light garment" and higher consciousness reality of 5D New Earth.

TWO

Earth School Orientation

The Earth School, a term I first read about in *Seat of the Soul* by Gary Zukav, is an evolutionary playground for advanced souls from all over the multiverse. The multiverse is made of many universes, or universities, where souls project their consciousness into various forms to evolve and learn in many worlds and environments. Each planet is a separate school within the larger university with its own unique dynamics at play. You are an eternal being who has lived many lives in many forms, quite possibly on multiple planets, each one bringing its own unique lessons as you journey on the path of God-realization, the path of realizing yourself as God in form. As a seeker of knowledge and truth, you eventually discover that which you seek is seeking you, and, in fact, you ARE that which you seek.

This ancient mystery school, the Earth School, is a master school and has everything that a soul will need to achieve unprecedented growth, expansion, and mastery. For humanity, the course work is mental and emotion-based and is full of challenging twists and turns to make your journey unique and exciting.

Free Will

You have the freedom to choose your evolutionary journey. You are free to choose your thoughts, beliefs, and actions. You have a choice to be in service-to-self or service-to-all. As you grow in awareness of your inner realm, you have the choice to be a slave to fear or to transform your intentions and beliefs to align with spiritual truth and unconditional love and become a powerful Divine Creator in service to the higher evolution of consciousness.

Let us visualize a branching off of spheres of consciousness that extend from the original sphere of Source, a family tree of Light. Each sphere branches out to another smaller sphere as the limitless Light of Source is stepped down to other spheres of consciousness. Eventually, we would come to what we call your oversoul.

The oversoul sends out parts of its essence to experience different lifetimes. Your soul is one part of a grouping of souls that have experienced and are experiencing many lifetimes simultaneously. They have acquired vast amounts of information that are merged within the consciousness of the oversoul. It can be likened to the shape of a hand where the center of the palm is the oversoul, while the fingers are the individual soul aspects that merge with the center of the palm.

You As a Soul

I have chosen to use the word soul primarily in the book to describe the immortal individual lightbody that moves from the higher light dimensions into physical bodies. It takes on limitations and karmic lessons so that it can know itself but is not impure or unholy. The impurities lie in the different layers of the lightbody such as the mental, emotional, etheric, and physical layers which are reconciled through spiritual practices.

While the English language can use the word in a variety of ways, both poetic and technical, I have tried my best to use the term specifically and with intention. When I am speaking of the True Self, I am speaking of the highest identity of the individual which is the pure Consciousness, Source itself. While there seems to be many beings, many souls, there is truly only One Light of Consciousness, your True Self.

At a certain point, your individual soul came into being. As a soul, you possess the ability to incarnate into different life forms to experience Creation and grow spiritually. You have lived many lifetimes and have learned many lessons in many forms. Some lifetimes are on the Earth, and some are likely in other forms in other planets, star systems, and universes. Many souls have been bound to Earth's negative karmic lessons for many lifetimes, experiencing the same cycles of suffering over and over, similar to a student who fails a class and has to repeat until passing.

As we come into the Earth life, we pass through a veil of forgetfulness (*avidya*/ignorance) and lose conscious memory of other lifetimes and the knowledge we gained from those lives, and we begin to fall under the spell of the seductive quality of the world of form, believing it to be real and that we are separate from The Divine.

Human babies are extremely vulnerable and fragile and are dependent on their caregivers to give them all their basic needs. Since we forget our connection to Source and our spiritual Self, Earth life is extremely challenging as we innately struggle to remember the truth of who we are. The light that we came in with often begins to fade as we become enamored with the illusion. We quickly absorb and adopt the limiting beliefs of our family and culture and quickly forget the light that we are.

Because of our spiritual amnesia, we begin to create a false self, an egoic identity structure that we piece together from the thought-forms and programmed conditioning that are available in our environments and experiences. Because of this amnesia and the chances of developing negative karmic patterns, only highly advanced souls choose to come to the Earth School.

Understandably, we get stuck in loops and karmic cycles, having to see the same themes and scenarios play out again and again until we have done enough research to understand, integrate, and choose the appropriate direction that aligns us with Higher Truth.

It should also be mentioned that many new souls are incarnated on the Earth directly from the Source having never had previous incarnations here. This is an experiment being implemented to assist the planetary ascension. These beings bring bright, fresh energy to the Earth. They have no previous karma and have a higher baseline vibration because of this. This helps to raise the overall vibration of the planet. These souls can also have a difficult time here on Earth because of all of the density held by humanity at this stage.

Soul Family

Soul family are souls that incarnate together, again and again, to help each other along their path of spiritual growth. Sometimes we play certain roles in one lifetime and switch in the next. We have scheduled rendezvous with different soul family members that activate us on our path of remembering. Sometimes it is pleasant, but often the initiations are painful and activate wounds within our consciousness that want to be healed through spiritual and emotional work. This "clashing," whether physical or psychological, is essential as it reactivates unprocessed energy for integration, spiritual insight, and assimilation of wisdom from life experience. Often the closest soul family member decides to play a "villain" in our story, or they may bring conflicting situations for us to learn from and have the experiences that we need to evolve.

Spiritual Council: Your Light Team

Prior to incarnating from the spiritual realms, you sit with a council of other light beings to design your next incarnation. These light beings, your council of guides, are highly developed spiritual beings that guide you through your incarnations. Some have lived human lives. Some have lived in other star systems that you are connected to. Some are Ascended Masters and angelic beings that no longer need to incarnate to learn and now mostly stay in the higher realms to guide and support the evolution of Creation. These spiritual allies are non-judgmental and eternally patient. They are behind the scenes coordinating rendezvous with other important people on your path and guide you through situations using signs, synchronicities, internal promptings, and other experiences.

Contracts

Before incarnating, you meet with your council of guides to create your contract for the next incarnation. This higher plan for your life is where you decide what emotional themes you will explore and which experiences will initiate you into deeper wisdom in that life. You decide the parents that will give you the conditions and genetic coding that will form the foundation for your life. In doing so, you are aware of the culture, spiritual and religious affiliations, sex, economic status, geographic location, etc. Each of these categories are like sub-classrooms, filters that we get to experience our unique human life through. I often chuckle when I hear someone say, "I did not choose this!" when, in fact, they are the ones that envisioned and signed the contract!

All is designed and planned, pre-chosen so that you have optimal conditions to grow. In truth, we have no one to blame for the conditions of our life but our own self. Suffering is not a divine punishment but fertile grounds for tremendous spiritual growth through contrasting experiences.

Each lifetime's experiences and knowledge feed into and support the other lifetimes as the soul advances through various consciousness stages. In fact, all of us have lived many lives in preparation for this Grand Transformation of Life occurring on the planet NOW!

Primary Guide

Everyone has a primary guide who stays with them for the duration of their lifetime. The other members of your council are skilled in the areas you are studying and have wisdom to share. Sometimes, these guides shift partway through a lifestream when someone shifts into a different area of learning and needs different guidance.

Once we incarnate, our guides communicate with us in many ways, mainly through our Inner Being. You are constantly receiving transmissions and signs from your team and Higher Consciousness. Learning to listen to your internal guidance happens naturally as you begin to tune into your inner experience, emotions, variations in thought quality, and so forth. Learning to quiet the mind is essential in learning how to communicate with your individual team of Light.

The uninitiated individual, a person who is not spiritually awake and aware of the other realms and the Family of Light, is mostly unaware of the guidance that comes to them. As you begin to awaken, you will notice increasing signs, synchronicities, and symbolism that seem to lead you down the Higher Path. Your guides speak to you through the matrix by sending these messages. They work with other guides of the souls who are beneficial for your path and growth and help to coordinate rendezvous opportunities through impressions broadcast into the thought and emotional fields of a person to offer the opportunity to follow the intuitive guidance.

It is up to each of us to discern what signs come from our guides, felt through the heart, and which come from the duality-based ego. Guides will not interfere with our free will, and their guidance is always loving and never fear-based, although they can transmit a strong impression if the timing is important or urgent. Your guides can see opportunities and events coming down your timeline before you experience them. Your guides will repeatedly send you the same information until you get it. If you miss it, rest assured that another opportunity will come to you as your team coordinates another chance to learn that lesson or take that step. When you receive the guidance, acknowledge it, send gratitude, and follow the guidance.

Non-Emergency Divine Intervention

For non-emergency assistance from your guides, you must ask. By asking from the heart, a simple prayer for divine assistance gives your team of guides permission to work in more areas of your life in more profound ways. As a sovereign creator, you have the authority to grant this permission. Simply ask for divine assistance and trust that much is happening behind the scenes already to assist your growth and healing.

Some may be open to light beings but may be closed to the idea of having guides from other worlds. The opposite is also true. If you have not, invite your entire team to be with you to assist. Ask your star lineages to assist you. Ask your Inner Earth family to assist you. Ask your angelic light being team to assist you. Welcome your entire lineage, past, present, and future to assist you on your great Mission.

There is great love for you out there, but they cannot interfere, and they will not approach until you have opened yourself to be reconnected. Intend that only the highest beings of Love and Light can work with you and open yourself to be reunited with your Family of Light! We have created the *Quantum Launchpad* course to help you grow in multidimensional awareness and develop your relationship with your Guidance Team.

Exiting the Earth School

When a soul finishes a lesson in the Earth School, it graduates to the next appropriate course of study. When a soul is finished with all that it came to experience and grow through, it is time to leave the body and continue the evolutionary pathway.

Multiple exit plans or physical death experiences are agreed upon depending on which way the life progresses. Many people exit earlier because they run their bodies out of vital energy and accumulate so much suffering because they do not learn their lessons which manifest as illness, disease, and suicide. Therefore, it is important to do spiritual practice to maintain the vessel as you explore your coursework.

As the incarnated soul approaches an exit opportunity, it decides whether to make adjustments to its approach towards life and remain, or else exit and continue its evolutionary path in another form. We can see the physical death experience as a graduation event. When a person leaves the Earth School, this means that they have learned all that they could in this life or have accomplished their life purpose and must continue the eternal path of soul evolution. Truly, you are an eternal being and no one really dies.

Stepping Out of the Body

When clients review the physical death experience of a previous incarnation in the IQH sessions, they are immediately relieved as they transition out of the body from the physical Earth realm and into a parallel spiritual plane of Earth that people call the Astral Plane. If others are around the body as they transition, the soul often wishes them to release the sadness because they feel so good now that they have left the body. For the most part, souls are greeted by a loved one who has already transitioned or a guide or spirit animal, something they trust as loving, and they are whisked away into the Light for healing and rest in the higher light dimensions. In some wisdom traditions, they describe different processes of this transition phase but in my sessions, it always seems much simpler.

There are times when a soul does not continue to the Light. Maybe they died suddenly or were heavily sedated and not aware that they left the body. Maybe they fear punishment from God because of fear-based religious beliefs. Maybe they have "unfinished business" and want to stay close to the physical plane to accomplish what they wanted. For whatever reason, some souls or portions of someone's essence such as etheric and astral debris do not transition and linger in the lower astral realm close to the physical Earth plane.

Spirit Attachments: Implants

There are varying opinions on whether it is the entire spiritual emanation that sometimes stays behind or only some etheric and astral debris that remains. To avoid making a blanket statement either way at this time, I can only confirm that sometimes some part of a lifestream does stay behind and can be problematic for my clients if the debris becomes attached to the client. Once removed, the problematic conditions fade away instantaneously or over time.

Many people are surprised to find out in hypnosis sessions that they have other energies attached to their systems that do not belong to them. Negative spirit attachment can happen when a person is in deeply traumatized or depressed states, habitually uses drugs and alcohol, or has in some way invited the energy into their system because of loneliness or another reason that weakens their energetic field. Disincarnate souls and/or parasitic astral thoughtforms use this as an opportunity to attach to the host and live out their "unfinished business." They feed off the light of the host and torment the consciousness and emotions of the person by creating self-sabotaging, obsessive-compulsive patterns. Often, the way the spirit died or illnesses they had when they died begins to redevelop in the host body. This is why energetic hygiene is crucial for every person to learn to maintain clarity and sovereignty in their vessel.

There are times that malevolent extraterrestrial beings install "implants" in a person's physical or subtle energetic bodies to track or limit the consciousness of the host body. Not all beings are in support of free will for humanity and seek to control and limit human consciousness and the restoration of our DNA. Most of the time, as I dig deep enough into the subconscious of the client, I find that on some level, the client unconsciously invited the experience to support their growth in some way.

Many beautiful beings on the planet assist with spirit transition and implant extraction in these cases. I have done it many times while clients are under hypnosis. We ask the Higher Self how it got there, how it affected the human, and what they have learned through the experience. We call in light beings, often Archangel Michael and Archangel Raphael, or a guide or loved one to assist the extraction. Every soul must go into the Light to continue the evolutionary process. When I help them transition, there is a huge relief, and they often wonder why they waited so long to rejoin their Family of Light. The effects are felt instantaneously by the client.

This is not to say that one should automatically blame negative extraterrestrials, entities, or curses for the conditions of their life. It is an opportunity to reclaim the sovereignty that you lost through your unconscious creation patterns. It is up to you to heal the parts of your consciousness that allowed such an experience. To release the resentment for such an "attack," send gratitude to the being(s) for creating conditions for optimal growth and release them to the Light. You can call on Jesus, the archangels, or any other ascended Light-consciousness being to assist you with the extraction

Some people, even after an entity extraction has taken place attract another entity attachment soon after because they have not effectively repaired their Lightbody or because they continue to enact the same patterns that caused the interference to begin with. It is up to the individual to repair their bodies and fortify their consciousness to maintain a clear vessel.

There Is No Hell

As mentioned before, there are resting places and healing temples for a soul to be refreshed and clarified once it returns to the higher light realms. After the soul is recharged and revitalized, the soul communes with its council of guides to review the previous life. This is done with grace and is never from judgment. During the review, plans are made, and preparations begin for the next life.

Every soul is welcomed back into the Light of Source. Never once during any of my sessions has a client gone to Hell or seen the "devil." These are fear-based, dogmatic control systems generated by superstition and tyranny to enslave humanity and feed off its fear. Even the most terrifying souls are received with grace and allowed to reflect, heal, and grow. Nothing is judged. The worst of the worst are simply recycled back into the Light for new creation. It is all part of the eternal evolution of Creation within the Divine Plan of Source.

I have heard of a place in the higher dimensions created for and by the souls who feel they deserve such a place. A "hell building" was created for them to play out their distorted belief systems until they decide to finally release their attachments to negative polarity and exit their self-inflicted hell matrix. The client said all who pass the building send prayers and loving intentions, inviting the souls to rejoin their beloveds in celebration of Eternal Life. How else would our Family of Light tend to those are suffering?

Some will reject this idea because on some level they still operate out of the belief of a fear-based reward and punishment system. We all contribute to perpetuating this system each time we act out of fear or teach a child to be afraid or ashamed. We see sin and darkness in the world because it still exists within the collective of humanity. We remove the "evil" from the world by removing the distorted, limiting, fear-based beliefs within our own consciousness first. Then we can assist others in liberating themselves from their own hellish creations.

We must stop blaming Satan, the devil, the Cabal, the negative ETs, the governments, and so on for the suffering on this planet. We have all played a part in adding to this horrifying imbalance that we see upon the Earth. In some way, we have all given some level of our creative power away and have allowed our bodies, minds, and planet to be corrupted and polluted. It is time to reclaim our light and reclaim this world through fierce love and unwavering focus. No savior will fight this battle for us. We ARE the second coming of Christ upon this planet, and we are the Children of God who will tip the scales and reclaim this world in Truth, Love, and Light!

Let it be so! Let it be NOW! Let it be in pure love!

THREE

The Human Experience

When a body is born, the physical body is given a soul. Newborn babies come in with fresh Light, fresh from the Source, and inspire joy in those around them as they emanate this pure Light and Love. I have had clients experience themselves as the consciousness of the sperm racing towards an egg surrounded by other sperm. Most of my clients who experience the birthing process in an IQH session see themselves with their guides preparing to come into a physical body as the embryo forms within the mother. Periodically they "pop in" to check on the development of the embryo or to feel into the environment the mother is experiencing to start to feel the sensations of physicality. However, the soul needs to be in the body by the time the body takes its first breath.

Sometimes being born holds such an intense trauma that it affects that incarnation for a long time. Coming from realms of Love and Light into a loud, cold, and sterile hospital room and all the procedures quickly done to a baby leaves an imprint with that child that stays with them for a long time, possibly several lifetimes. I had a client with shoulder injuries from where forceps gripped her shoulder as she was born. She recalled the scene with full detail. By re-experiencing the origin of the pattern, she released the imprinted effects of the trauma from her body and associated mental patterning and began to heal instantaneously as the pressure and pain released from her shoulder, neck, and head.

Entering the Earth Matrix

Human bodies are bio-transducers, organic machines for receiving, transforming, and emitting subtle energy. When a child is born, it immediately begins to absorb data from its environment. Sensory information like sounds, smells, physical sensations, and the emotional thought-form vibrations of those in the birthing space begin to inform and develop the mind of the new human. We are dropped into the simulation, and we begin to download data immediately.

Souls entering a new physical life need sacred high-frequency environments to enter the Earth plane. While some souls may choose a traumatic birth experience to learn a karmic lesson of some kind, these souls deserve to be received with love and calm energy to honor their passage from the higher light planes to the Earth plane. They are like sponges absorbing all the new information through their senses. When a child is young, we can protect their pure energy and vulnerable minds by creating harmonic environments for them to come into their own brilliance. They should be masters of their bodies and minds and fully aligned with their Inner Source. They should be guided into their multidimensional mastery so that they can be all that they came to be!

Termination of Pregnancy

Part of the draw for spiritual beings to descend into a human body is the vast experience that can be had through physicality. Some babies decide partway through the birthing process that, for whatever reason, the conditions are not right for them to fully incarnate. Earth life is dense and can be too intense for some. Some souls choose to stop the incarnation process during labor or a few days after birth, deciding it is too harsh or that merely being born was enough to complete their contract for that life.

From a higher perspective, some people manifest a pregnancy as an alarm alerting them to bring more conscious awareness to the state of their life's conditions or to change the direction of their lives. This is a nexus point for all parties involved as to which path they want to follow. Sometimes the choice is between allowing the pregnancy to continue or terminating the pregnancy. There is no judgment for women who choose not to carry their pregnancy full term. Everything comes down to intention. Will the person use this as an opportunity to follow a higher path or use it to continue with the momentum of their previous attitudes and perspectives? Everything is held with perfect love from Source and is seen as a learning experience for the souls involved.

A pregnant woman came to her IQH session to connect with the soul that wished to incarnate. The woman had decided that she was not ready to bring new life into the world. Through hypnosis, she connected with the consciousness of the unborn child to explain that it was not time. The next day the woman had a powerful experience during the medical procedure where her guides surrounded her and an angelic light-being form of a young girl came to share that she would be her daughter in the future. The experience was full of love and grace.

Source's Love and Grace is unwavering. We, as humanity, place our own ideas of morality and judgment onto choices and expect that the Divine would hold the same harshness that we do. Where we stumble, we have the opportunity to grow in humility and grace. Each choice is an opportunity to learn and listen to the higher guidance of compassion.

Even if there is no judgment from above for having an abortion, abortion often creates suffering. To avoid such suffering, we can learn to discern our life choices and live a noble life. Our bodies yearn to be treated as holy temples for the indwelling of spiritual light. To end the suffering related to sexuality, it is important to honor the act of sex as a powerful, sacred container for spiritual transformation and pleasure. As we come into higher consciousness and practice sacred sexuality, we will move beyond needing to manifest experiences like abortion to learn through suffering. Tragic experiences of sexual trauma are echoes from our past, often originating in past lives. Victims of violations such as these likely have a set of beliefs about themselves and fears that they hold that draw such terrible experiences into their lives. While it may seem cruel to say, this has been demonstrated over and over again in the quantum healing sessions.

In the Earth School, we often learn through suffering. Deep spiritual practice and healing will help the person understand the nature of their suffering to avoid subconsciously recreating the experience in the future. Remember this is a school of karma and it is through suffering and the redemptive power of love and higher knowledge that we break free from endless cycles of trauma.

Domestication and the Human: The New Gods of our Reality

When we are first born, we seemingly get everything we need from our parents or primary caregivers. They are responsible for feeding, clothing, and keeping us safe. They appear to be the source of love and resources, the god and goddess of our own personal reality.

These seemingly omnipotent beings can bless us or curse us at will. We learn to obey the gods and give them what they want so that we can continue to be in their graces and receive their blessings. They are the law of the land, and we learn quickly that it is best not to question their authority or knowledge. At this point, we are young and small, and we learn that there are limitations to our power and that we are dependent.

Part of our awakening process is the repatterning of our identity in connection to our biological parents. They were, fundamentally, our entry point into the Earth School and laid out the necessary conditions for the themes we would explore in this life. Emotional courses not completed in our family of origin play out in our other relationships as we grow older.

When we look at human behavior, we can separate consciousness into a few archetypes or "parts" that regulate how we process life events and relationships.

One archetype is the Child, which is made up of the spontaneous joy and intuition found in the innocence of childhood. The Child can also be a Wounded Child which has difficulty processing big emotions like when children have emotional meltdowns and fears related to authority figures and the stressors and desires of life. The Adaptive Child is the immature part of our consciousness that we created to protect our Wounded Child by rebelling against opposing forces or by changing our feelings and behaviors to fit in.

The Parent archetype is a fusion of all of the authority figures of our life, especially our birth parents. This parent can either be loving and supportive or critical and threatening.

The Adult is the mature part of our consciousness that handles life with a mature and rational attitude. The Adult is responsible for regulating the needs of the Child and the authority of the Parent.

We are constantly jumping between these archetypal vantage points. When someone is in their Child, they can inspire the Child in another, bringing more spontaneity and joy into the interaction. Meanwhile, the Wounded Child can bring out the Critical Parent or Adaptive Child in another. The Adult mediates between the two so that we do not stay in our Child and avoid the responsibilities of life and lets "bygones be bygones" by cultivating openness, practicality, and understanding to move forward in life without staying in the critical perspective of the Parent.

Our true parent is Mother Father God, the maternal and paternal emanating qualities of Source. Instead of spending our lives trying to fit into the karma of our family identity and ancestral trauma, we can rise above this and synchronize with our True Parents. As we emulate and embody their Love and Wisdom, we truly become Children of God. We can listen to all of our different "parts" and mature and integrate them into a cohesive unity and rise as Children of the Most High.

This idea of multiple "parts" to our personality expands when we start to factor in mental patterning stored in our subconscious from our personalities and experiences from other lifetimes, personality traits passed down through our ancestry, as well as flashes of insight and thoughts from our higher consciousness identities. We are each a collective. We are not one personality but a multidimensional, multifaceted conglomerate of many parts.

Some of us were born with siblings who are also doing what they can to receive affection and resources from the adults. At some level, a competition ensues. We begin to learn the human experience of scarcity consciousness as the attention of our source of love and resources is divided amongst the siblings and activities of life.

Our "family of origin" sets up the dynamics of how we relate to the rest of the world. Much healing is needed by all of us concerning our family of origin and our ancestral lines. Each new life is an opportunity to bring fresh light into the family tree to soothe ancestral trauma and evolve beyond the momentum of ancestral karma. We all took on our portion and it is up to us to fully heal our lineages through our own transformation.

We are like erasers being born into the Earth matrix with a frequency of love and a heart filled with devotion. A fresh chance to grow light! Advanced souls incarnate into the darkest regions of the human drama to bring Light and Wisdom and to transmute generations of shadow and distortion. These beings are fierce angelic souls who will use their liberation from suffering to serve humankind by transforming their suffering into wisdom.

Developing Your Matrix Character

Learning how to use the body takes time. It takes months to learn how to roll over, crawl, sit up, and eventually walk and run. This is vastly different from our spiritual body that can change form and fly! From the moment we are born, we begin to absorb the conditioning of the world through our senses. We are taught that this body is "me" and that it belongs to a family, a religion, a race, and a nation. We are given a name, gender, and an identity based on our body and cultural customs and learn that the body is subject to harm and, eventually, death. We begin to cling to physical life and our body and believe that this is all we are.

The world around us and our experience in it leaves its mark on our physical body. All of this is encoded into the muscles, into the breathing patterns, habitual holding patterns, intonation of our voice, eye patterning, fascial grid, and all the way into the cells and DNA. Everything is recorded and translated onto the body. This is how we take on family traits and hereditary illnesses, social posturing habits, accents, biases, preferences of our community, and so on.

The Human Language

The human family that we were born into has a particular language to describe its experience and share information. These words are made up of collective agreements of what each word means. With those also come individual agreements of what the individual uses the words for. Definitions for commonly used words like "love," "god," "good," and "bad" are all understood differently by different people and social groups. The meaning of words even changes over time from generation to generation.

Words carry power and intention that transform consciousness. Every word we speak or think ripples subtle information across our consciousness, affecting every level of our mind, body, and spirit. As we create sentences, we weave spells that crystallize and focus our NOW experience and draw forth a reality that matches the vibration of our inner and outer dialogues.

Many of the words in our language and how we use them are rooted in negatively polarized consciousness. When we speak half-truths, curse at someone, or intentionally use our words to cause harm, we immediately lose life force energy. We poison ourselves with our own words and thought patterning.

As we become more aware, we can feel the words' vibrations and use language that supports restoration and unity. We can develop a new vocabulary to describe our awakening life experience and use our words, thoughts, and intentions to create a new story of our personal and collective future and reverse the spells we have placed on ourselves through our distorted thoughts and words. Let us be dream-weaving wordsmiths of the New Earth and create a magical reality through every thought we generate and every word we speak!

Cultivation of Belief Systems and Belief Structures

As we learn the language of the land and the emotional and mental associations with each word, we also begin to take on our family and culture's belief systems. As we imprint the association and emotional patterning associated with the word, these become our beliefs.

The adult humans told us what our name was, what their name was, and told us our relationship to them, and what that means. We believed them, came into agreement with it, and adopted the information as truth. We learned the agreed-upon names and labels and applied them to everything in our experience. We began to narrate the story of what we were experiencing through these predetermined definitions and associations, and we programmed our consciousness to perceive things in a certain way.

As we grow, our human experience is programmed through beliefs passed down through family, society, and various institutions. These beliefs are reinforced by other programs and reward/ punishment systems. When we are "good," we get affection. When we are "bad," we get punished. Some lessons we learn through traumatic experiences leave deeply embedded thought-forms and beliefs in our subconscious, operating mostly in the background of our awareness. For example, if we were bitten by a scared dog as a toddler, we may have a subconscious belief that all dogs are dangerous.

You can think of these subconscious beliefs like applications on a smartphone, silently draining your power, speed, and proficiency from your device. Once we become aware that there are open programs no longer useful for our path, we can use various tools to "close them down," so that we can use the power of our awareness to perceive life clearly without the distortion of limitation.

Ego/Personality

When most people think of who they are, they think of their personality, thoughts, and physical body, the bodymind complex. They identify as their past experiences and behaviors, thoughts, family identity, national identity, age, sex, gender, religious identification, and so on. All these experiences are temporary and contribute to developing the personal egoic identity structure. Some people consider the ego to be "bad" when, in fact, the egoic identity structure, when entangled in the conditioning of the world, is made of positive and negative qualities. When I use the term ego, I am referring to this limited egoic identity structure. We can use spiritual practice to mature our consciousness beyond limited identification into universal I AM presence. We can make friends with the wounded part of our egoic identity structure and use higher knowledge and wisdom to bring our consciousness into appropriate perception and the realization of our higher consciousness identity.

The lower egoic identity structure is developed by us to protect our light and being, preserve our identity role (self-image), and keep the body from suffering or death. The conditioned ego, the separate self, is mostly made of protective, fear-based limiting beliefs. This is the part that thinks it can be "good," "bad," "sinner," "holy," and so on. The ego is concerned with protection, the accumulation of power, and self-preservation. The egoic identity structure creates hierarchies of importance and power and gives value to certain experiences over others. The illusion is so real that most people do not look beyond this level of identification.

Some religious institutions threaten people with eternal damnation or punishment from God if you begin to question and think of yourself as being any more than a lowly human, a servant, and a slave who is stained for eternity. This belief system feeds that shadow aspect of our personality and traps us in cycles of suffering.

Each of these identities (e.g., boy, son, husband, American, etc.) within their respective communities comes with certain beliefs and agreements of how a person should behave, think, and feel. These agreements are reinforced by reward and punishment systems to enforce the programs. This is a duality-based system, and it is what humanity has been operating in for thousands of years. Even the Godhead is seen through this duality program and is portrayed as a vengeful punisher. One must be "good" to get to Heaven or else spend eternity in Hell. This is a control system that is out of alignment with the ever-loving Divine Parent.

When most people refer to "I" or "me," they are likely speaking about their body-mind complex, their psychophysical self. The Buddhists break the bodymind complex down into five *skandhas* or five aggregates. This includes the physical form (body), feelings and sensations, perceptions and recognitions, thinking processes, and our mind-consciousness. All of these are subject to change. They arise for some time and dissolve, yet there is another part that witnesses all of these manifestations and changes occur. This is your True Self which is ever free, perfect, and whole. It exists beyond all names and forms. It is beyond all worldly identities, labels, and beliefs, yet we quickly cover it up in our early life through mental conditioning and the hypnotic power of the experience of being in physical form and taking on the spiritual amnesia of humanity. Regardless of our awareness of it, this pure existence consciousness is always there shining in the background of our experience.

Relationships

Relationships in the 3D consciousness are about control and power. What many people consider to be "love," with a lowercase "l" is a self-satisfying control system where both people expect the other to behave a certain way to win affection. From the seemingly limited supply of love and sensory gratification, we behave in ways to manipulate our external reality in an endless search for fulfillment and happiness. As we start to awaken to life's interconnectivity and begin making choices for the Greater Good of All, we begin to transform our relationships through higher expressions of unconditional love and heartfelt understanding. We begin to cultivate a richer inner life as we cultivate self-love and compassion for others. We begin to release the control programs from our own consciousness and empower others to be their own source of joy.

Emotions

Our emotions are our guidance system. They let us know what we like and what we do not resonate with. If we do not have the skills to work with emotions in a healthy way, our emotional realm likely tortures us in endless cycles of clinging, aversion, desire, and fear.

In our pre-awakening phase, our inner desires and our outer expressions do not match. We may be afraid to show our true emotions and may become deceitful out of fear of rejection or ridicule. Sarcasm, denial, avoidance, criticism, niceties, and aggression may be used to maintain a false sense of security and public image. We may repress, restrict, and reduce the expression of inner desires, judging them as "good" or "evil." In doing so, we develop a false sense of value. Self-aggrandizement, self-pity, and self-loathing are all symptoms of a degrading spirit as we play pretend and maintain our self-image.

In an immature consciousness, we may have specific conditions for us to show love and compassion. Our relationships may have different levels of honesty, authenticity, and transparency to manipulate the other person to do what we want and maintain our outward appearance. We may silently beg for approval and validation from those with whom we relate and unconsciously audition people to play out our own inner world's subconscious roles.

In the belief that fulfillment comes from our external world, we may become territorial and hoard items and money to stockpile our external power. Consumerism is fueled by the misperception that true joy and power come from our external world's conditions. There is no end to this appetite, and continuous accumulation of wealth and materials will never fill our inner void.

Many people have monotonous lives, avoiding the mystery of uncharted paths because they learned to "go with what they know" to maintain happiness and power because it is "safe." This primitive animal instinct keeps them unevolved and immature in their own emotional, mental, and spiritual growth, having to never face any new challenges or reflections.

Some people develop superstitious beliefs in their attempt to control life. They may hope that if they do "this" or "that," they will earn God's Love or get a ticket to Heaven, or at the very least, avoid misfortune. Each of these beliefs keeps us in states of shame, judgment, and powerlessness. These beliefs cut us off from the experience of God's Love, the fullness of the Self, that is always available to us. Let us learn to drop deeper than the mind and the limited conditioning of the egoic identity structure to feel the deeper part of ourselves that is always in connection with the Higher Power so that we may learn to work in unison with universal law and rhythm to create beyond our perceptions of limitation.

Society

As we zoom out, we can see how separation consciousness and lack mentality are outpictured in our collective societies. We can begin to see how systems of control based on fear and misidentification are at the core of all mainstream institutions and hierarchies. In the denial of our interconnectedness and inherent connection to the Divine, we have created systems of enslavement, domination, and oppression.

Across the globe, an elite group of extremely wealthy and powerful people forms a web of shadow control over the life and consciousness on planet Earth. Some may call this the "Deep State" or the "Cabal." In the time of this writing, this horrific system of abuse is beginning to be exposed as much of the world is beginning to awaken to the truth of what is and has long been occurring here.

The main instruments of mind control are the media, medical, and education systems. News stations and media networks use the problem-emotional reaction-solution pattern to steer the human collective into coerced consent and voluntary compliance with the service-to-self agenda of the elite and corporate interests. Mainstream media and smart devices have been used to induce people into an almost constant hypnotic trance and suggestibility. This takes less than a minute's worth of focus on a screen. Subliminal messaging and hypnotic suggestions are scripted into the video media programs, popular music, and advertisements to keep humanity at a certain bandwidth of consciousness.

The use of plant medicines and psychedelics was an integral part of my own "hacking" out of the matrix. I have an intuitive feeling that one of the reasons cannabis was cultivated on the planet was to assist us in freeing our consciousness from the mind control grid. Plant medicines, entheogens, and psychedelics are powerful tools for "breaking the matrix connection and can be used respectfully and safely to encourage consciousness expansion. The Controllers have created smear campaigns and legislation to keep these medicines from the people out of fear of what humanity would do when their mind has been set free.

The education system is used to program consciousness with a controlled narrative about history, mathematics, science, social behavior, and ethics. When the human collective reunites with the Star Nations and

Family of Light, we will get a much more advanced education that will make the current education system completely obsolete. What humanity clings to and calls science currently will look like baby blocks when compared to what the advanced intelligent beings from the stars and light dimensions use.

The "sick-for-profit system" uses genetically modified food, toxins introduced to the environment from chemtrails and industrial agriculture, toxic pharmaceutical drugs that remove symptoms but do not holistically heal, fluoridated water that corrodes the cognitive and nervous systems, onslaughts of vaccinations for newborn babies, and other means to keep people sick while charging money for the cure. Banking systems keep high interest rates so it is extremely difficult to get out of debt. This is especially true if you do not have health insurance and have to pay out of pocket for medical care.

Follow the money. Who profits from endless wars? Which families benefit from the mining and sales of fossil fuels? Who owns the central bank of your nation? As you follow the trail, it eventually narrows to a small group of people who control the entire planet for their own benefit, yet even beyond them in the higher dimensions exist forces that influence these dark masters. These service-to-self forces are being removed from the Earth, with the assistance of many great beings of light and advanced star nations, to liberate the planet and restore it to the paradise it was designed to be.

Many of the religions of the world propagate dogma based on damnation, impurity, and judgment. They deny our divinity and claim to be the only pathway to the Divine. These institutions enslave humanity, repressing and controlling the consciousness of the masses with fear and lies, and keep humanity from ascending to Higher Knowing. They take divine teachings and distort them to fit their agendas. If these institutions do not confess to their abuse of power, they will be left behind in the changing times as all who carry service-to-self consciousness will no longer be able to sustain life upon planet Earth as she transitions.

We are more than a biological machine having a temporary life. We are immortal, divine beings of light. The richness that we seek and the power that we desire are found by creating a rich inner life and relationship with our Higher Nature and Source. Ascension is the tool to lift us individually and collectively out of the cycles of suffering that we have created on the planet and move us into a culture that honors life as sacred.

Instead of being a culture focused on accumulating external wealth and power and avoiding physical death, we can be a culture that celebrates eternal living and the equality of all expressions of life. We can move beyond the misperception of separation and embrace the truth of our Oneness and Unity in the Light of Source.

Wheel of Karma: Samsara

The purpose of reincarnation is for the soul to be perfected by unconditional love and compassion and to grow in our relationship with the Divine. What we do not complete in one life, we will complete in the next. This continues endlessly until the individual soul has learned all the lessons offered through physical life.

Samsara is a Sanskrit word for the endless cycles of reincarnation, the Wheel of Karma, created by the loops of distorted thinking and the suffering mind. We step off the Wheel of Karma through practices of Ascension. We step out of the reincarnation loop by maturing our consciousness with spiritual knowledge and wisdom and reaching for the Light of the Divine. We avoid endless cycles of needless suffering by honoring our divinity and choosing thoughts and actions that support a Greater Good for All.

Humanity, as a collective, chooses to live in a hellish reality based on misidentification, distorted relationships, and the culmination of external power. Terrifying wars, destruction of ecosystems, extreme poverty, illness and disease, overflowing prison systems, unstable weather patterns, and humanitarian crises are all symptoms of collective denial of our divinity and the avoidance of the right relationship with our True Source.

Liberation includes releasing a victim and slave mentality. It is not the Church, the Archons (nonphysical controller entities), the Cabal, the Anunnaki, your parents, your lover, the government, and so on that is to blame. These are conditions for you to free yourself from the tyranny of thought. Wipe the mirror clean of illusion so that you can see the face of the Divine shining back at you. All is Self, all is God in manifestation seeking itself through the illusion of multiplicity and ignorance.

It is up to each of us to heal our inner world, push the upper limits of our consciousness, and ascend into the glory of our True Nature. If we want to see Heaven on Earth, we must refine our inner reality and open the pathways for the indwelling of Divine Light in our being. As we liberate our light from the enslavement of our distorted beliefs, we become way-showers for the rest of humanity to free themselves from the tyranny of thought, thereby dismantling the power of the controlling forces.

As we awaken to the Higher Love of the Higher Power, we become an extension of the Higher Evolution, and we begin to emanate the Love of Source out into the world. As each soul awakens to the Light of the Divine, they join the collective radiance of ascending humanity and begin to pull all of Earth life out of the shadows of fear and negative karma and into a brighter future and the dawning of a New Earth.

FOUR

High Alchemy of the Soul

Alchemy is the practice of transforming energy from one form to another. Alchemy is commonly understood in stories of turning water into wine or simple metal into gold. High Alchemy, the alchemy of the soul, is the transformation from mundane consciousness to the discovery and embodiment of one's True Divine Nature. This process activates and accelerates as the Mysteries of Creation and Laws of the Universe begin to be revealed to the honest seeker of Higher Knowledge and Wisdom of the Divine.

All alchemical processes need a container for transformation. The alchemical container for high alchemy is mindful awareness. Mindfulness is the practice of bringing our life's gross and subtle manifestations into the light of our awareness. Nondual awareness is the ability to see beyond the illusion of duality and see with the eyes of loving awareness. The spiritual alchemist uses mindfulness to observe limiting beliefs and patterns to refine distortions and misperceptions with compassionate understanding and spiritual knowledge.

Divine Embodiment

As we awaken and transform our worldly conditionings and limited thinking, we begin to embody the Light of our Divine Nature. Divine embodiment is a process of spiritual evolution where we give form through our beingness to higher spiritual virtues and anchor the Light of our True Nature into our human form. Every moment we can use self-inquiry and self-reflection to understand the origin of our thoughts and actions and what fuels our intentions in life. From this vantage point, we can discern which intentions, words, and actions are a reflection of our pure consciousness and which impulses come from our unprocessed trauma and worldly conditionings.

Manifestation

Manifestation is the process of bringing nonphysical energy into physical creation. Our life circumstances are a manifestation of inner experience and the intentions we carry, many of which are buried in our subconscious mind. As we awaken, we reclaim our powers of Divine Creatorship and become deliberate creators. As we take our power back from our subconscious limiting beliefs, we begin to attract higher manifestations at increasing speeds.

The magic behind manifestation is vibration. When our dominant vibration is high, our mind is fortified by love and higher truth and we attract more of what we want and experience synchronous events as we begin to see how the matrix of Creation works. When our vibration is low and our mind is infiltrated by distorted perception, we experience little to no synchronicity and attract manifestations that reflect those limiting beliefs and unprocessed traumas which create our inner distortion.

Our intention, our inner resolve, drives and motivates our path of creation. As we start on our awakening path, we become aware of our inner experience and refine our beingness into its highest golden nature and expression. We begin to manifest higher and higher creations and draw forth our own version of Heaven on Earth.

The Journey of a Thousand Miles Begins with One Step

The hero's journey is a framework of spiritual evolution found in many stories of beings who have pushed the upper limits of their consciousness and abilities to reach a higher state of exaltation and freedom. This is a path of initiation where a being departs the old ways to pursue higher knowledge, wisdom, and experience.

The hero or heroine's journey consists of three stages:
1. The Departure where the initiate leaves the known world and crosses the threshold into the unknown.
2. The Initiation phase is where the initiate must face challenges and grow into a higher version of themselves.
3. The Return phase is where the initiate, having been transformed into a new expression of themself, brings the mystical elixir, the wisdom of their experience, back home to be used as a force of healing and transformation for the good of all. Let us look more closely at each phase to understand the mystical journey a bit deeper.

Departure: The Call to Adventure

All quests begin with a call to adventure, an inner yearning to journey beyond the horizons of what is currently thought or experienced and be initiated into higher awareness and understanding. It takes surrender and trust to follow the initiate's path and truly "Know Thyself." To choose awakening means to release attachment to all you have known and identified as. It takes nothing short of bravery to awaken.

Many hear the call and are afraid to leave the mundane behind, hoping to snooze for "just five more minutes." This is likely due to fear, a sense of duty or obligation, insecurity, or any other limiting or self-sabotaging beliefs that keep people from taking a leap of faith into uncharted territory. Some people will live in perpetual states of suffering for long periods of time because they do not believe they are capable or worthy of the change and growth they desire. Awakening is a choice that is constantly asking to be renewed as we become increasingly more aware of our inner realm, actions, and the repercussions of those actions on our life.

Awakening means taking full ownership of the circumstances of our life. Many would rather stay in a victim mentality of negatively polarized consciousness than accept that their life circumstances have been chosen and created by them, mostly unconsciously, for the purpose of spiritual growth. Many would rather stay in their story of suffering and "play it small" than take brave steps to make new choices and face the void of the unknown. Many hear the call, but only the brave embark on such a mysterious journey of high alchemy.

An Honest Prayer

On some level, the consciousness of the individual petitions the Godhead/Universe/Light/Spirit to show them the truth, and they send out an honest prayer or plea from the heart. This reaching for something higher is a crucial step in the initiation process. This prayer comes when one has experienced enough of the issues that have manifested from protecting the ego and personality. All the ways of "going it alone" have become exhausted. Often the emotions have become so painful that a person humbles themself and calls out from their heart to be shown the Truth, to be shown The Way.

From here, Spirit begins to work with the consciousness of the being to mature it to a sovereign, divine embodiment.

Supernatural Aid

Once the adventurer decides to accept the call to journey into the unknown, a seemingly serendipitous event occurs where a guide, physical or nonphysical, appears to point the initiate towards the higher path. Maybe it is someone who has information or resources that point to more wisdom and keys to unlock the mysteries. Maybe it is a dream or vision that activates the person and encourages them to seek out more information. Maybe it is a series of signs and synchronicities that are hard to ignore. I highly recommend watching the movie, *The Matrix*, which has many keys for awakening. The supernatural aid in this movie is when Neo, the main character who questions the nature of reality, receives a message that the Matrix is real and is invited to a meeting where he can learn about the truth of the reality matrix he is trapped in.

Threshold Guardians

The Threshold Guardians are the forces that attempt to keep the adventurer from following their path. Maybe this shows as relationships that try to control you or sow seeds of doubt, shame, guilt, or fear for desiring to expand beyond what is currently known, accepted, and experienced. Maybe it is the journeyer's limiting, self-sabotaging belief structures that keep them from taking the step towards a new way of life. These are just obstacles on the path of mastery and the initiate must truly trust their path and intuition and believe they are worthy of receiving the benefits that growth brings. If they succumb to the inner shadow or the pressures of the outer world, they will inherently experience more limitation and suffering until they follow the call. Once they affirm that they are ready and forge onward on the path less traveled, the magic of transformation can truly begin.

Initiation: Crossing the Threshold

Every person has a unique story to share about how they began to awaken. Every one of them is beautiful and powerful in its own way. Maybe it was gradual, maybe it was sudden. Maybe it was gentle, or maybe it was traumatic. Maybe it was practical. Maybe it was mystical. Everyone who begins to awaken has some initiation experience that points them towards a higher destiny pathway and a higher consciousness reality. These events, people, and experiences activate within them the desire to "know thyself." Slowly, the layers of misidentification peel away as they begin to deprogram their consciousness and ascend out of the limited cultural programming, ancestral trauma, and personal identifications, aversions, desires, fears, and attachments.

When one decides to seek the Mysteries and higher consciousness and steps beyond the default paradigm, they will be tested to measure their commitment to their sovereignty and awakening path. Some people may be threatened by new ideas and unusual behavior and try to lure the new traveler back into the old world, their old character, and limited egoic identification. This is just a test for the initiate, an opportunity to trust their inner guidance and inner knowing and take action towards their higher ideal expression and true liberation.

Trusting one's inner voice of wisdom and reason is the foundation for the path of spiritual growth. Awakening involves honoring the inner voice of Spirit and releasing habits that give our power away to outside authority. Heaven/God is within each of us, softly guiding us towards everything we have ever wanted. We are always being presented with the same option: acknowledge and follow the presence and guidance of the divine felt within or follow "The World" and outside authority. One leads us to salvation, the other keeps us in cycles of suffering and endless reincarnation cycles.

Mentorship: A Guide to Show the Way

As we begin to awaken, we start to look, consciously or unconsciously, for a teacher or mentor to guide us to higher truth. All good teachers, true teachers, point us back to the power we have within our beingness, to the "teacher that lives within." These mentors are role models for qualities that we want to mirror and embody. It is important to keep in mind that all beings are equal, and we risk disappointment when we put our teachers on pedestals. Many "spiritual teachers" on the Earth plane will reveal their own shadow as we move further along the ascension pathway. There are many teachers and spiritual leaders who use spiritual knowledge and their influence as a teacher to fulfill service-to-self agendas. Hidden agendas are hard to hide in an increasingly telepathic and intuitive culture. All of us are subject to our humanness and all hidden agendas will eventually be brought into the light of awareness.

Once we have learned all that we can from one teacher, we move to the next teacher. We are meant to use many teachers in our life path, and we limit ourselves by devoting ourselves to one teacher or guru. In truth, everyone and every life circumstance is our teacher.

The message that we received through clients is that "They," the spiritual beings that tend to the development of Earth and humanity, have coordinated it so that there will no longer be one source of divine wisdom and prophecy on the planet because the "Savior" and "Guru" templates cause people to lower in vibration and give their power away. Instead, "They" are spreading the dissemination of spiritual information and insight across the globe through many people to keep a higher balance. Anyone or any group that says that they are the savior or that only they know the divine truth is likely using this to generate fear or manipulate people for their service-to-self agenda. The true teacher lives within, and no outside authority supersedes your innate connection to the Divine.

Initiations: Trials and Errors

Each relationship and life circumstance is a course in spiritual growth, an educational alchemical container for transformation. The coursework involves understanding our emotions' hidden meaning and bringing more awareness to our thoughts, habits, beliefs, and actions. As we move through a course, we experience certain conditions to stimulate the potential for spiritual growth, consciousness expansion through trials and tribulations, and the insight these experiences bring. Every moment is ripe with the potential for deeper awareness and spiritual growth as one begins to consciously transform into higher consciousness. If we do not learn the lesson, it comes back around again in another circumstance or another relationship.

Helpers along the Journey

At certain points in the initiation phase, helpers appear on our path to encourage our growth and expansion. Sometimes it is pleasant and sometimes the relationship is challenging. As we awaken, we start to see our relationships as catalysts for spiritual growth. We begin to grow in our awareness that what we judge or fear in another reflects our inner world. Many people leave one relationship, only to manifest and recreate the same circumstances in another relationship. When you are in a spiritual relationship with another, you see the other as an ally for spiritual growth. As we shed the victim mentality and take authority over our experience as Divine Creators, we see that the biggest villains in our life, especially the characters involved in the most painful experiences, served as powerful activators for massive healing and consciousness expansion. It is up to each of us to cultivate a compassionate heart so that we can tend to our wounds and realize the deeper teachings of our traumas.

Growth: New Skills

Each challenge in our life is an opportunity to grow spiritually. We can use alchemical practices to transform our stagnation, stored trauma, and limiting beliefs. We can read literature that inspires higher thought and understanding. The more we use our skills and acquired knowledge, the better our life becomes and the more automatic and integrated the new understanding becomes. Questions lead to more questions as we come to a deeper and deeper understanding of our True Self. True nourishment is that which feeds our soul and sets us free.

The Abyss: Ego Death & Spiritual Rebirth

The Dark Night of the Soul is a spiritual crisis period for an awakening initiate as their old identities and beliefs go through a death process. This is a deeply transformative phase as the light is seemingly stripped from the world. Deep churning, pain, doubt, fear, and grief often color the experience of this Dark Night. The Dark Night of the Soul finishes as the initiate discovers the light within them and begins to embody a higher expression of themselves. Rising like the phoenix from the ashes, they emerge with deeper insight and wisdom. Miracles are simply a shift of perception from fear to higher love and unity. When we release our addictive thinking towards fear and discover the source of safety and abundance found within, we begin to access our power as divine creators and limitless beings.

Final Changes

Once we are finished with one course, we move into a higher-level course to achieve a better understanding. We see this outpictured in the changing of relationships, jobs, homes, and so on. Often, right before our "graduation," a final test, a final opportunity emerges to see if we are truly ready to move into the next level of consciousness exploration. We are meant to change and grow. Some people may have a difficult time accepting that you act differently or have new boundaries. While it may be uncomfortable, this is simply a test to see if you are truly committed to embodying your deepest truth or if there are still places in your consciousness where you get hooked into old patterns that need to be reconciled before you can be fully anchored in your new embodiment. It is in this phase that the initiate receives revelations that illuminate the mind to higher truths that liberate their consciousness and create a higher perspective of their life. Finally, the sword is pulled from the stone, and victory has been achieved! Now the victorious adventurer can begin their quest back home.

Atonement: Reconciliation

As we awaken, we may find that we have harmed someone else when we were caught in the illusion of our ego or a less enlightened state. It is important to make amends and reconcile with those we may have wronged. The best way to make amends is to transform your limiting beliefs and stored trauma that caused the suffering. From this place, you can approach the situation with the intention to relieve the suffering of others. Reconciliation involves healing the hearts of all parties involved and coming to a deeper understanding. To love others as we love ourselves effectively, we need to first love ourselves unconditionally. Grace is available for all, no matter how terrible the action is.

Ho'oponopono is a Hawaiian healing practice for reconciliation and forgiveness. It can be translated into four steps and phrases: "I am sorry, I love you, please forgive me, and thank you." When we say "I am sorry" to another, it shows that we have thought about our actions and see that we have potentially caused harm to another. We say "I love you" to let them know that we release the fight and want positive solutions for all involved. When we say "please forgive me," we invite them to be a part of the healing process. They may also want to confess their role in the issue. We say "thank you" because we have come to a deeper understanding of how this opportunity provided nourishment for our growth.

We do not need the other person to forgive us to release ourselves from feelings of guilt. That is our wound to heal. When we do our part of the work, we release our part of the karma with this person and can truly stand in sovereign support of the other's growth. We can do this process for loved ones far away and even those who have traveled beyond the physical world.

A Gift from the Universe

When we complete our missions, there is often a gift from the universe for persevering through challenges. Maybe it is a physical item, an opportunity to share your new skills or talents, or some other blessings of abundance from the universe. Facing your inner shadow is tough work! Being sure to thank God/the Universe for blessing you will open the pathways for even greater blessings!

Return Changed

"We only keep what we have by giving it away." is an adage from 12-step programs that perfectly describes the final stage in the cycle of the hero's journey. As we learn to make peace with our inner distortions and transform into the limitless nature of our Divine Self, we stand as emanations of Higher Understanding and Higher Love. We broadcast this frequency into the world through our very being. We then carry within our essence a healing elixir, wisdom that can be shared with those who seek a higher truth. It is our responsibility to humanity to share our spiritual insight and discovered gifts. Our heroic characters from humanity's history were pioneers, rebels, visionaries, and artists who pushed the upper limits of what was thought possible to achieve the seemingly impossible.

From their new heights, many have borrowed strength and inspiration to walk their own path of initiation. Each of us carries these extraordinary potentials within us. Each of us can be pioneers of consciousness that help to unshackle the collective of humanity by first taking the shackles off of our own self.

May these words shared here fuel your path of liberation, your own hero's journey, so that you can bring back the wisdom you have discovered within and share it as medicine for this world.

FIVE

Awakening in the Matrix

As we begin to awaken to the Light and Love of Source, to the Light of our soul, we awaken within the dream we call life. This awakening process is called Ascension. During this process, we question everything we believe. We begin to sort through all our internal rubble to uncover the Divine Self that lives within. This process begins our exodus from the mundane mainstream consciousness and initiates us into the Mysteries of Creation. We "save" ourselves from our karma and mental trappings by reaching for the Higher Knowledge of the Divine. This reaching for higher understanding is crucial to begin the process of awakening and ascension.

As a new initiate, we begin to notice the programming in the people and world around us. The illusion loses its luster; the games we used to play and roles we used to act out do not interest us as much. Many of us have felt completely alone as most of the world is focused on the material reality and egoic preservation and not the spiritual quest. They are asleep within the dream. This is perfectly fine as every soul designs a time when they will begin to awaken to their divinity and the Higher Realms of Light.

This awakening process is well on its way for millions of people around the world. What once was only available for the mystics, sages, and spiritual masters throughout time is available for all people who desire to grow in Light and Love and evolve into higher, heart-centered consciousness. Can't you feel the quickening of transformation occurring in your own life and across the planet? While some look at the conditions of the world and see destruction, others look and see a healing crisis as all of humanity faces its karmic shadow. Nothing can stay hidden anymore and all will be brought into the Light as we shift into New Earth reality.

Quantum Physics is now beginning to measure that the multiverse is conscious and interconnected through a unified field through principles such as quantum entanglement and nonlocality. We are beginning to measure how matter is affected by our consciousness and how all of life is connected in a symbiotic relationship. These advancements will continue to accelerate as humanity's consciousness expands and ascends as we connect to a higher consciousness reality through the upgrading technology of our bodymind complex.

Everything Is in Support of Your Awakening

You are the writer, director, and main actor of your dream. How you think and what you think about changes your reality. Your environment is constantly rearranging to match your intentions, vibrations, and desires. Whether you know it or not, the entire universe is conspiring in your favor for your victory in awakening to your Divine Self. Even in the moments of your deepest pain when you feel that you have totally fallen from grace, you are still building massive momentum towards attaining your ascended self-mastery. Every experience is valuable, and every experience carries nourishment and spiritual wisdom to fuel your awakening. This journey is about YOU and your willingness to unconditionally love every part of yourself and extend that radiance out into the world.

Different Levels of Consciousness

In the Ascension community, we speak about humanity's ascension in terms of "dimensions" or "densities." There are likely other models to describe this transmigration process of our consciousness and this world into the higher consciousness reality of New Earth. Some say that Earth is moving from third density to fourth density and that humanity is becoming a fourth-density collective. Some say Earth and humanity are moving from the third dimension through the fourth and into the fifth dimension. I understand and find value in both ways of describing the process. I will summarize both perspectives from my understanding to provide a framework for the discussion of Ascension.

The first time I heard of ascension in terms of "density" was through a somnambulistic client who described the creation process of the multiverse and the evolutionary pathway of Gaia and humanity. This client's Higher Self referred to the Operation Terra material that the client had read that activated his awakening process. The material is said to have been channeled from the Heavenly Hosts and is strikingly similar to what has been channeled through the quantum healing sessions. I recently read parts of the Operation Terra material that speak about the differences between density and dimension. Here is a much simpler summary of that information infused with my own understanding and experience.

When we think of ascension in terms of changing "density," we are talking about shifting the material reality's particle structure by increasing the vibration of the material. This is understood easily by water's transformation from ice to liquid water to water vapor. As more energy (i.e., heat) is applied to the material, the density begins to shift from solid matter to a vapor that you cannot necessarily see but can feel.

We can think of the shift from Third Density to Fourth Density as shifting bandwidths of reality, similar to Dorothy from the Wizard of Oz where Kansas is seen as a black and white film reality and Oz is the bright technicolor reality where magic is real and anything is possible. We are shifting to a whole new "program" of a harmonic Earth reality that is beyond anything we can comprehend from our current vantage point.

In Third Density Earth, our current Earth, we experience the physical world in the three dimensions of space: height, length, and depth, in a linear experience of time. As we start to awaken, our experience of time begins to shift and become nonlinear as we tune into the unfolding of eternal time.

In Fourth Density, we have the previous four dimensions as well as the Eternal Quantum Consciousness and experience ourselves as extensions of the Oneness of Creation. This moves us out of linear thinking and linear time experience into multidimensional awareness experienced through nonlinear holographic consciousness.

Another way to think of consciousness evolution in terms of "densities" is to think of different complexities of consciousness forms. In First Density, we see inanimate objects such as fundamental energy, elements, gases, stones, and minerals. In the Second Density, we see organic animate forms like microbial life, plants, and animals. In Third Density, we see physical beings such as humans with their individual consciousness and intellect. In Fourth Density, in terms of human consciousness evolution, we see individual consciousness operating in universal consciousness which gives humanity tele-thought communication with Earth, the Earth kingdoms, nonphysical and nonlocal beings, and Source. There are other densities beyond Fourth Density, but I do not feel they are necessary to explain for this book. I am sure that there are many ways people categorize and describe "densities," but this is a simple enough theoretical model to understand what people are talking about when they speak of consciousness evolution in terms of "densities."

Humanity, in its current form, cannot experience Fourth Density because we have a Third Density body. Christ Jesus (Yeshua ben Joseph) brought the template for the Fourth Density human back to humanity through his ascension processes and soul mission. His birth, life, death, and resurrection laid the foundational template to restore humanity and the Earth to its original divine blueprint and perfection. Humanity's transformation from the Third Density human body to the Fourth Density Adamic human template is already underway and experienced as ascension symptoms as our DNA is returned to the perfected divine human template.

Now let us shift to another way that people commonly look at this Ascension process in terms of dimensions which is the most commonly used and understood framework for understanding the process of Ascension.

3D Consciousness: Slave Mind — Living in the Material World

In 3D consciousness, we perceive ourselves as a single point in the world, cut off from everything else. We are ignorant of our higher consciousness identity as a divine being and create a false self based on cultural programming and societal structures. This ego is fear-based, operates in survival mode, and can be quite animalistic in its expression of self-preservation, domination, and control.

In 3D consciousness, we perceive life in linear time via the five primary senses through the untrained mind's duality. Life is seen as finite with a string of events that follow each other, seemingly unrelated. We can have a "slave mindset" and "victim consciousness" and give our power to the world outside of us. From the 3D perspective, our biology decides our destiny, and we see ourselves as victims of our past and enslaved by our genetics, culture, and economic status. It is a "me versus them" reality that focuses on controlling the physical elements of life to feel safe, secure, and powerful.

All the Earth issues at this time, all the imbalance and shadow, stem from this core wound, this belief that we are disconnected from the Divine. This suffering and misinformation have been amplified by distorted religious teachings that use shame and guilt to control the consciousness of that religion's followers. As humanity awakens to its divinity, all imbalances will fade away as we return to the truth of our Oneness with All That Is and rise in our embodied consciousness as divine beings of light.

4D Consciousness: Initiation of Light and Vibration Stepping into the Magical Reality

As we awaken, we move from 3D consciousness into the initiatory passageway of the Fourth Dimensional Consciousness. 4D Consciousness is like stepping into a world of magic. The matrix of Creation begins to speak to you as signs and synchronicities begin to emerge on your path. It is like the background comes to the foreground as you begin to sense the spiritual and mystical significance in your life. Events seem to be interconnected as you begin to see the patterns of the matrix reality. This is where an ascending consciousness begins to recognize universal laws like the Law of Attraction — "that which is like unto itself is drawn."

The initiate begins to take inventory of their internal experience and find higher compassion to transform and alchemize the inner realm of their consciousness. The seduction of duality begins to fade away as Unconditional Love begins to show The Way. The default belief systems of the collective consciousness born from limitation, trauma, and unconscious karmic programming, begin to lose their power over our consciousness. We begin to awaken within the dream of Earth and reclaim our sovereignty as Divine Creators with free will.

The Higher Self is a term used by spiritual circles to describe the part of our consciousness guided by Divine Love and Wisdom which maintains an unbreakable connection to the Higher Realms of Light. For the sake of this text, the Higher Self is described as this mature part of our consciousness that is always seeking harmony and works for the betterment of All. It expresses through flashes of insight, intuition, inner knowing, discernment, ethical action, and universal compassionate connection.

To transition from 3D to 4D and beyond, one begins to become curious about the Divine and their connection to the Higher Worlds that exist beyond the five senses. Through this curiosity, the Mysteries begin to be revealed to the seeker. The seeking initiate begins to follow the internal "still small voice" and moves into higher states of enlightenment. Some call this inner guidance the Holy Spirit, their Higher Self, or their soul. In truth, there are a few Higher Selves, higher consciousness identities, which exist in higher and higher light dimensions connecting to the Source. This is reflected in the physical world through the pathways of connection from humans to the solar system, the galaxy, super galaxies, and the Great Central Sun. As above, so below.

This Higher Self consciousness, or the illuminated, mature part of our consciousness, guides us away from our False Self, egoic identity, into our higher exalted True Nature. As we release the limited lower mentality of the ego and collective default belief structures and step more and more into our sovereign power as divine creators, we begin to merge with a higher consciousness that can perceive beyond the visible light spectrum and open to information from Higher Light Realities and Consciousness.

In 4D consciousness, we begin to awaken to the subtle energy universe of spiritual light and subtle vibrational frequencies and begin to consciously and/or unconsciously activate and repair our Lightbody. Our empathetic nervous system begins to activate as we begin to sense and feel subtle energy fields within and beyond our physical form. There are many schools of thought on the study of the human subtle energy systems which each have their way of accessing, manipulating, and reconciling the energy systems.

This energy system can be activated, cleansed, and strengthened through spiritual practice and proper diet to prepare it for its transformation into the next "light garment" of the perfected divine human template with fully activated and repaired 12-strand DNA.

For this process to complete, all vibratory fields, every atom of the human body, is to be brought into a state of sustained coherence and harmony which naturally occurs through the integration of ascension energies, focusing one's life on spiritual values and love, and eating a proper diet that is free from toxins.

5D Consciousness: Cosmic Christ Consciousness — Moving into Miraculous Reality

The oversoul is a higher aspect of our consciousness beyond the psychological, neurological, and physiological process of our human self, existing beyond the physical nature of reality. Once we awaken and repair our Lightbody through diligent practices and spiritual growth processes, we begin the process of linking with our Overself consciousness and the overlay of the Overself Lightbody. This process was demonstrated publicly by Christ Jesus (Yeshua ben Joseph) and is written about in the *Tibetan Rainbow Lightbody teachings* and the *Lightbody Ascension Teachings of Ancient Egypt*.

Fifth Dimensional (5D) consciousness, Overself Consciousness, or Christ Consciousness can be described as the perspective of reality experienced as the eternal unfolding of heavenly and miraculous phenomenon witnessed through loving nondual awareness. When humanity ascends to and maintains 5D Consciousness, we will be completely aware of our connection to All That Is. We will no longer experience the lower emotions of fear and suffering. We will instead maintain loving awareness and the deeply profound and embodied knowing of our interconnectivity with all of Life.

Oversoul Embodiment: Multidimensional Awareness

In 5D consciousness, we are fully immersed in our body's ecstatic blissful awareness as an avatar for the higher consciousness of our oversoul. The oversoul consciousness contains all the wisdom and experiences from our other lifetimes. Each soul emanation returns with life experience after each incarnation and merges with the total wisdom of the oversoul consciousness. Once we completely "dock" with our oversoul consciousness, we will have access to all the knowledge and wisdom from our current life as well as other lifetimes in our oversoul's collective experiences and legacy.

Wayshowers are those who have been developing their consciousness, moving out of the standard 3D consciousness into 4D consciousness to shine as planetary ascension leaders. They have continued to push the upper edges of their spiritual development so that they may guide others along the path as the masses begin to awaken. These beings are great Cosmic Masters who are proficient and experienced in moving planets and species into their next evolutionary phase. These lightworkers have lived lives as master healers, cosmic frequency technicians, quantum space engineers, architects of reality, angelic light warriors, Ascended Masters, goddesses, oracles, and quantum consciousness pioneers and have come from all regions of space-time and beyond to assist humanity and planet Earth. All of the best are here upon this Earth, and surrounding it as well, to welcome the dawn of this new day!

The Three Stages of Spiritual Awakening

The journey to New Earth involves surrendering to unconditional love and learning to live in harmony with Creation. This involves striving to "know thyself" and awaken to the redemptive power of compassion, forgiveness, and understanding. Through healing and spiritual processes, one activates and maintains the Higher Love vibrational perspective of their Higher Self and opens themself to the Higher Mysteries of Creation. Through our desire and efforts to grow and mature in our love and appreciation of the Divine, we begin to embody that love and become honorable, cooperative co-citizens of the cosmos.

This awakening and ascension process can be broken into three segments of *purging, activation,* and *embodiment.*

We are healing and releasing all the limiting beliefs, stored trauma energy, and toxins from our physical body and subtle bodies during the purging phase. As this old energy leaves, we move into the activation phase. We become more in tune with subtle energy, our Inner Being, and our spiritual gifts during the activation phase. As we move into higher thought and follow our guidance from our Inner Being, we embody the presence of our Higher Self, our radiant Divine expression of pure Light.

This process is accelerated by spiritual practices that purify and unite the body, mind, and spirit. A "practice" is anything that we repeatedly do to accelerate our healing and transformation consciously. Homeostasis is our body's natural ability to return to perfect balance and health. Homeostasis, perfect balance, is the natural state of our body. We can use spiritual practices to support our systems back into balance, health, and coherence.

Spiritual practices align us with our Higher Self and anchor us into multidimensional presence. We can be simultaneously aware of our physical, etheric, emotional, mental, and spiritual processes at any given moment. As we bring more mindfulness to these processes through our practice, we are more likely to be aware of them in other areas of our lives to consciously make choices that align with our highest path.

Conscious embodiment practices help us to grow in our capacity to be conscious and present in our bodies. Physical practices like meditation, yoga, qi gong, walking, dancing, running, or somatic practices like Feldenkrais or Pilates bring our awareness to the present moment as we train the mind to focus on the subtle processes of our body, mind, and energy. These meditative practices help us slow the mental processes down to feel more grounded, centered, and present in our subtle energy field and our life.

Cognitive therapies, reading of self-help and sacred texts, journaling, and other practices bring more mindfulness to our mental processes so that we can become aware of limiting perspectives and train our minds into higher thought patterns and habits. Breathing practices help us clear old energy from the body, train our minds to the present moment, and bring fresh energy into our body to support natural, vital flow in our systems.

There is an infinite number of practices available to soothe your system and align you with your Inner Being and higher consciousness. They do not have to be "spiritual" to be effective. What matters is that we have activities that we do consistently to help us gain positive momentum in the direction of our higher goals and aspirations to holistically embody our Higher Self.

Beyond bringing mindfulness to all these processes and finding coherence in the body, it is vital to have an openness and desire to connect with the Higher Consciousness Reality to make this evolutionary leap of Ascension. Rejecting the Divine or holding animosity towards the Divine closes the crown and heart chakras which connect us to the evolutionary energies. The opening to and development of a closer relationship with the Divine Consciousness opens the pathways for Higher Light to saturate the human bodymind instrument with a higher evolutionary coding. This moves the human body's biology out of patterns of decay and entropy into a Higher Evolution of Eternal Light and Eternal Living. As this Higher Light enters the biofield, it enters the cells and DNA. It begins to repair the building blocks of the organic material so that the full brilliance of one's consciousness can express through the physical body's genetics.

Shifting Paradigms

In the default model of civilization, power is something outside of ourselves, and we see ourselves as separate from everything else. We are limited to our five basic senses, only able to prove and believe in things we can see, touch, taste, smell, hear, and measure. We have created a whole civilization based on controlling our external world to feel powerful and secure. This is a devouring power that is opposite of the true nourishing and life-affirming power of the Divine. The New Earth paradigm invites us to perceive the world through energy and our Inner Being's guidance. We discover that the power is within us, and we had it all along. Even if we cannot see the connection, we can feel that all of Life is interconnected and One.

Spiritual awakening, the ascension pathway, is an ongoing process of shifting paradigms. When you change the way you look at things, things will change the way they look. We can see this shift happening not only on a personal level but at all levels of civilization. Having forgot our True Nature, everything we have created in the 3D matrix was created from an inverted, limited perspective and misidentification. Everything we have thought to be true and everything that we created from that limited perspective will shift as we transition to the New Earth higher light spectrum reality.

When paradigms are shifting, it is normal for us first to reject new information that contradicts our current paradigm, our current way we interpret reality. Eventually, we may come to accept some part of the new perspective, even if we are not ready to fully accept the totality of the new paradigm. Eventually, we become more and more accepting of the new perspective's components, gradually embracing the new beliefs and new ideas. There is no going back to the old ways from that place, and we move forward in life with a fresh, updated framework of understanding.

The New Earth paradigm is absurd to many people and likely sounds insane and based in fantasy. It does not matter if everyone believes in extraterrestrials, Ascended Masters, or even God, all at once. It makes sense that most people would reject these concepts at first since most reject their own divinity and light. Instead of focusing on getting people to believe in the abstract and foreign concepts, we can focus on guiding people into their hearts and allowing the Higher Love to show The Way. This is why Jesus and the disciples focused on the heart as an access gateway to the Absolute Reality of the Higher Realms of Light.

We are each like a baby bird about to hatch. From within our egg, we believe that the world is only the inside of our egg. As we crack through the illusion and break free from the shell, we realize that the world is so much bigger than we could have ever imagined from our previous perspective.

As we shift into New Earth, the new consciousness, and the repaired and upgraded Lightbody, all the systems based on the old paradigm must fall away and be replaced by creations made from the new paradigm of our individual and collective expanded consciousness. This means a complete transformation of how we relate to ourselves and the world. This also means that every part of society, our governments, financial systems, medical systems, and educational systems must have a complete overhaul to match the new paradigm.

As this world decays and the New Earth emerges, many will fight to keep the old ways alive. This is futile as every atom of life on Planet Earth will be reset and revitalized through the powerful undulating Light emanations from the Great Central Sun. The potency of these transformative divine powers is amplified by the compassionate efforts of our extraterrestrial, ultraterrestrial, and positive subterranean allies joined with the thoughts, prayers, and actions of awakening humanity upon the Earth.

YOU are here on Planet Earth, our beloved Gaia, with a BIG purpose! You are here to awaken to the truth of who you are, an aspect of Source, a Divine Being. Through the process of this realization of your Divine Nature, you become a conscious bridge between Heaven and Earth, a walking prayer, and an ambassador for the Light of Source. You are the bridge between the Higher Heavenly Light Realms and Earth! This process is about you bringing all your shadows into the Light to be healed and growing in your capacity to allow the Love of Creation to flow through you and illuminate this world.

Self-Initiation Prayer

Moving into the higher consciousness is a personal choice made by an individual who desires to know the Mysteries and truly "Know Thyself." Different traditions have different ceremonies or rituals for initiation into the Mysteries. I invite you to enact your own ceremony that is deeply personal and a symbol of your personal exodus from the mundane world into the Hidden Mysteries. You can create your own or follow this prayer I have designed.

1. Set up a ceremonial and sacred space for yourself. This may include lighting some candles and turning the lights down low, maybe burning incense or diffusing your favorite essential oils. Some people prefer silence or light, ethereal music. You can create an altar with symbols and pictures that represent Higher Love and the Divine. Let your intuition and creativity guide the way.

2. Sit with yourself in quiet, mindful awareness and connect with your

heart by bringing your hands to a prayer position or by resting the hands on the heart center. Gently extend and equalize all the breathing stages: inhalation, pausing, exhalation, and pausing to calm the mind and bring it into the present moment.

3. With your intention, welcome the Light of the Divine to be with you. Imagine, sense, and feel this Light completely surrounding you. Invite your spiritual guides, angelic light beings, and loving ancestors to be with you. Feel their love as they gather around you. This may be the first time you have ever consciously reached for them, yet they are always with you and always shining their love upon you. Since this is a free-will planet, you must ask for them to work with you. Once you have initiated communication and connection, they will be able to work with you in a much more expanded way that is beneficial and appropriate for your path. Simply intend to connect and trust that the connection has been established.

4. Use your voice to make a statement and declaration to the Universe/Source/Family of Light that speaks to your decision to follow Unconditional Love and the Light of Truth.

Beloved Father Mother God, Source of my Being, Light that I am:

- I choose now to awaken in my consciousness to the Truth of Who I Am.
- Open my eyes to the Greater Love Light and the Higher Mysteries of Creation.
- Open my heart and show me The Way of Eternal Peace, Eternal Life, and Eternal Light.
- Awaken and reform my DNA and make my body an instrument for the indwelling of spiritual Light.
- Let me be a lamppost for the seekers of your Grace and Wisdom so that all may find liberation from cycles of suffering.
- Let my words and actions dispel darkness so that I may be a luminary in this world and beyond.
- I surrender my personal will to the Higher Will of the Divine and choose to live a life guided by Unconditional Love in service to the Greater Good of All.
- Infuse my consciousness with higher vibrations and the power of awakening and ascension.

- Let me commune with the Family of Light and Star Families so that I may be a bridge for many worlds of Love and Light and an extension of the Higher Evolution of Creation.
- Activate my full potential as a realized Divine Being and help me be a powerful Light Force in the liberation of all beings from cycles of suffering.

Let it be so! Let it be Now! Let it be Love!

5. Take some time to sit quietly and feel the vibrations and sensations of your Inner Being. You may even feel inspired to dance or sing a song to celebrate your initiation. When you are finished, continue with your day and trust that you have activated your sacred path of Ascension.

SIX
Universal Laws of Creation

You are a powerful creator with the ability to manifest your own Heaven on Earth. You can break free of karmic cycles and create the life you truly desire. You need to be aware of a few rules to get the most out of this Game of Consciousness. Once you understand and apply the rules of the game, you will launch yourself on a much easier path of creation. The origin of the teachings of these principles/laws (on this planet) can be found in the ancient texts of Hermetic Philosophy and other occult and esoteric schools of thought who received these teachings of universal knowledge from the higher realms and higher consciousness beings from beyond the Earth.

Below I have described a summary of my understanding of some of the basic Hermetic philosophical principles that have helped me on my path of High Alchemy, the alchemy of consciousness. I highly recommend the classic text *The Kybalion* by Three Initiates if you wish to journey deeper into Hermetic philosophy and further activate your mastery in alchemical multidimensional creation.

Law of Divine Oneness (Law of One)

All is One, and One is All and everything is in THE ALL. Everything is Source. All of Creation comes from one Source. All of Creation exists in a continuum of descending movement from and ascending towards the glory of the primordial Source. Nothing is above or below in value. Nothing is separate, and all of Life is connected in a symbiotic relationship in the Unified Field of the One Source. Nothing exists outside of the One Supreme Source. In fact, the Advaita Vedanta philosophy would say "All is not, Source IS" as all names and forms appear within Source.

The One Being manifests itself in the illusion of multiplicity. In truth, there is only one of us here! We can use the appearance of multiplicity or duality to understand the deeper wisdom of the Oneness of All and to truly "know thyself." Every time we choose to see beyond the illusion of separation, we reaffirm the Truth of Unity and Oneness of what appears to be many but is truly ONE. The mantra of "I AM THAT I AM" opens our capacity to experience the Oneness. This same mantra is found in other languages such as "*Eyeh Asher Eyeh*" in Hebrew and "*Aham Brahmasmi*" in Sanskrit, which both translate to a similar meaning of "I am the all-pervasive, vast, limitless Supreme Source."

- If all is THE ALL and The All is One, is there anything in Creation that you consider "outside of God?"

Law of Mentalism

"Watch your thoughts, they become your words; watch your words, they become your actions; watch your actions, they become your habits; watch your habits, they become your character; watch your character, it becomes your destiny." —Lao Tzu

Everything in creation is a product of the Infinite Eternal Mind of Source. The Multiverse is within the mind of the Supreme Source and is continuously evolving through the evolution of divine thought. From the simplest evolution of subatomic particles to the most complex orchestrations of cosmic events, all is happening within the mind space of Source Consciousness.

This universal law is mirrored in humanity's capacity to dream, imagine, and evolve thought into new creations. As we think, we create. Thoughts are a manifestation of our vibration. When our overall vibration is high, we manifest enjoyable thoughts of inspiration, insight, and joy. When our vibe is low, our thoughts drag us deeper and deeper into our story of suffering.

In the words of Abraham-Hicks, "a belief is just a thought you keep thinking." Most beliefs are programmed from our cultures and upbringing, and many are based on doubt, fear, and control. Our beliefs are our Book of Law, and we use our Book of Law to discern, judge, criticize, and evaluate our experience. As we grow in awareness, we can consciously choose how to shift our thoughts in a more positive, life-affirming direction and rewrite our Book of Law. Spiritual awakening and self-mastery involve deprogramming these limiting beliefs and aligning our thought processes with Universal Truth and Wisdom.

Emotions show us the quality of our belief systems and how we process energy information from the world around us. If we experience negative emotions, we are processing the energy and information from our experience through limiting beliefs and possibly unprocessed trauma from the past. The Law of Attraction magnetically attracts a similar situation into our NOW moment to retrigger the unprocessed energy so we can process the information correctly and mature our consciousness.

If we experience unpleasant emotions and situations, we can turn inward to find out what within us is drawing this experience into our reality. *How have I created this? What is my part? How are my thoughts contributing to this situation? What belief am I holding that is out of alignment with my soul? What can I learn?*

Each thought and word spoken is a spell that we cast on ourselves and our environment. Are we working with white magic or working with shadow magic? Are we giving power to our light or power to our suffering?

- If THE ALL is Mind and Creation is mental by nature, what are you doing to guide your thoughts toward higher thought patterning that aligns with Divine Knowledge and Divine Creatorship? (e.g., meditation, reading sacred texts, mindfulness practices, forgiveness work, etc.)
- How can you deepen in awareness of the parts of your consciousness, shadows in your personality, which are self-sabotaging or limiting? What steps can you take to reconcile those "parts" to clear the mind of negativity and align it with higher truth and coherent thought patterning?

Law of Correspondence

As above, so below, as within, so without. The microcosm is a reflection of the macrocosm; the reverse is also true. What you experience outside of you is an out picturing of your beliefs and emotions of your inner experience. What is happening in the physical dimension reflects what is happening in the astral dimensions. What is happening in the astrological alignments reflects what is happening within our inner progression and transformation and so on. All of these reflections and presentations can be utilized for high alchemy to "know thyself."

- Where can you take more responsibility for the conditions of your life knowing that what happens around you is in some way a reflection of what occurs within your mind?

Law of Vibration

All of Creation is made from Light and Vibration. Everything moves and vibrates in circular patterns. Everything is energy, and nothing rests. These pulsations of energy are the building blocks of all phenomena of our reality and beyond. Different aspects of Creation have different vibrational rates (frequency) that give them a unique vibrational signature. Physical objects, feelings, thoughts, and sensations all have their unique frequencies.

Distorted energies, limiting beliefs, and unprocessed trauma are entropic. They take away vital life force and creative vision and move us into a downward spiral of decay, a lower vibration. Source Energy, the Ein Sophic Light, is the highest, purest form of Love and Light energy with the highest vibration. It is the energy of centropy, harmonic evolution, and balance. When we align with life-affirming values and beliefs, we begin to put out a higher vibration. When we cultivate a Source-driven intentional life, we live longer, happier lives, and everything and everyone around us benefits from that vibration as we become an extension of the regenerative energy.

Our vibration and energy signature are constantly in flux due to many forces that affect our vibration. The food we eat, the environments we are in, the people we are around, the thoughts we think, and even our simple intention in each moment create immediate shifts in our vibrational output. As we become sensitive to subtle energies, we begin to grow in discernment of what we attach to and what we release that is not serving our higher aspiration of self-mastery.

- Knowing that all manifestations on all planes of Creation are vibrational, how can you use your will, the power of focused thought and intent, to raise the frequency of your manifestations? What actions can you take to clear out and reconcile lower vibrational energies to raise the frequency of the bodymind complex, your environment, and your manifested experiences?

Law of Perpetual Transmutation

There is the saying that "the only thing constant is change." Everything is in a constant state of change and evolution. Nothing stays the same. All experiences arise, abide, and dissolve in a continuous state of transformation. We, and everything in the universe, are constantly receiving, transmuting, and transmitting energy. We see this in the cycles of the breath, the stages of our life, the change of the seasons, and so on. Everything is meant to evolve and transform. Everything is evolving in a constant dance.

This is good news for someone who is experiencing something negative and painful. Having faith and KNOWING that everything will change eventually is sometimes all that is needed to shift someone from a low-vibrational, limited perspective to a higher, more enjoyable state.

- Where do you hold fixed judgments or negative internal images? Where do you hold yourself or others in limitation? Where are you static or holding yourself back from evolving? How can you use this Law to allow thought to evolve beyond its current preconceived notions and assumptions and into openness and higher understanding?

Law of Polarity

Everything in Creation has an opposite. Everything in the physical, mental, and emotional realms has a dual opposite. There are two sides to every coin. There are two ends of a stick. Everything is, and it is not. For every problem, there is a solution. We know what we do not want because we know what we do want. Life is full-spectrum so that each side of the polarity can be understood more deeply by the opposite expression. In truth, the opposites of anything are truly the same but with varying degrees of polarity in expression which is interpreted through different points of perspective. What is a blessing for one person may seem like a curse to another. What is enjoyable for one may be uncomfortable for another.

The book *A Course in Miracles* defines a "miracle" as a change in perspective which fundamentally is a change of polarity in our understanding of a situation. We can consciously respond to uncomfortable or negative situations by reaching for higher, positively-charged thinking that empowers us as architects and manifesters of our reality.

Humanity has the choice of being in service-to-self (negatively polarized) or service-to-all (positively polarized). This polarity plays out in the realm of our personality when we behave in a way that serves our egoic identity or from a place of altruistic action that honors all of Life.

- Where do you hold negatively polarized perspectives (i.e., judgment, resentment, pessimism, aggression, etc.)? Using the power of mental alchemy, how can you move up the vibrational scale towards mental neutrality or more positively polarized perspectives (e.g., inspiration, empowerment, sovereignty) that are rooted in nonviolence and compassionate understanding?

Law of Relativity

It is what it is. Nothing in life has any meaning except for the meaning we give to it. Nothing is good. Nothing is bad. It just "is" until we filter our experience through our belief systems, compare it to other experiences, and project meaning onto it.

- How do you project meaning onto people, places, and events? Good? Bad? Holy? Loveable? Unlovable? Damned? Evil? These judgments, interpretations, and biases are reflections of your consciousness.

Law of Rhythm

Everything moves and vibrates in rhythms and patterns. We have seasons, anniversaries, heartbeats, weather patterns, music, life cycles, and so on. The Multiverse can be imagined as an orchestral masterpiece of symbiotic rhythms and patterns, with each sphere of creation having its own set of tones and layers within the symphonic composition of the Multiverse.

When we become aware of rhythms and patterns that are out of tune, out of harmony, we can shift our intention and attention and consciously choose to focus our energies in a way that establishes new rhythms and patterns that support balance and flow. When our negative rhythms are brought into the light of our awareness, we can practice patience with ourselves and our manifestation and use spiritual wisdom to guide us into a new rhythm. This begins a spiral pattern of change that diffuses the backward pull of the negative, entropic thought-form energy. Over time, with consistent influence from our practice of aligning with spiritual wisdom, we move forward into a new rhythm that builds more and more momentum in a positive direction.

- What are the triggers that take you into cycles of suffering? How can you use mental neutrality (Law of Polarity) to "step off the wheel" and create a new response and a new outcome?
- How can you align with Earth's rhythms and the astrological movements in a way that is intentional and sacred? Sunrise? Sunset? New Moon? Full Moon? Solstices? Equinoxes?

Law of Causality: Cause and Effect

Every cause has an effect, every effect has a cause, and nothing exists outside of this universal law. These words describe the interconnectedness of phenomena in manifestation across the physical, etheric, mental, and spiritual planes.

"Luck" and "chance" are words that are describing where one does not understand the cause. The concept of "luck" is a superstitious belief based on the limited consciousness of the Higher Order. Nothing happens by chance but occurs because of infinite inputs from infinite chains of events from the physical, etheric, mental, and spiritual planes which all lead back to Source, the original Cause to all effects.

Newton's Third Law of Motion states that there is an equal and opposite reaction for every action. There is a cause to the effect, and nothing is happening by itself. Every intention we carry and thought we think creates a response in one or more planes of Creation.

This law is sometimes called the Law of Karma. Karma teaches us responsibility, not morality. Responsibility can be defined as the ability to respond to our manifestation in alignment with the greater good and light of our inner Source. It is often mistaken as a morality system of good and bad. This perspective of karma is a duality-based control system that distorts the Eternal Love and Light of Source. There is no judgment from the higher realms, only grace and support in evolving to higher states of glory.

- Are there areas of your life that you have begrudgingly accepted that they will not change? Do you feel powerless in relation to the will of the government, your spouse, your boss, financial state, your family karma? How can you step off the wheel of karma, the wheel of suffering and ignorance, and take back your power as a sovereign creator? How can you be an agent of change in your own life and community?

Law of Gender and Divine Androgyny

Everything in Creation contains masculine and feminine qualities and attributes. This manifests on all levels and planes of Creation. Feminine energies are associated with receptivity, creativity, reflection, magnetism, and so on. Masculine energies are associated with action, willpower, electricity, and assertiveness. When the feminine qualities overpower the masculine, we may get stuck in receptivity and reflection without taking action. When the masculine energies of our personality and consciousness are strongest, we may act too quickly without considering and envisioning our options. Divine Androgyny is the balance, union, and harmony of masculine and feminine principles in our consciousness. As we heal and integrate all parts of our Divine Masculine and Divine Feminine qualities, we embody the Love, Power, and Wisdom of Source.

The Law of Gender in terms of the physical sex of a human is seen in both male and female bodies and reproductive systems. In terms of gender, we have many expressions of masculine and feminine genders in male, female, and intersex humans. Many starseeds and the new children coming in have spent lifetimes as androgynous beings and find it restrictive to try to fit into a polarized system. Our species is a kaleidoscope of gender expressions that should be acknowledged and celebrated!

- Can you identify the masculine and feminine traits of your personality? Are there any areas of your life where the polarity of these principles is imbalanced? Are there areas where you need to be more reflective, nurturing, intuitive, sensual, or still? Are there areas where you need to be more direct, firm, structured, or goal-driven?

Law of Abundance

We exist within a unified field of energy that is endless and eternal. What we experience within that field is a projection of our own beliefs and perspectives. When we are experiencing lack, we are in a state where we have cut ourselves off from the limitless field of Creation and the Higher Power. As we refine our vibrations and update our understanding of Creation, we begin to allow more of the higher manifestations of ease, gratitude, patience, trust, and love into our experience. As we open to the Higher Love of Source, we begin to work with the power that creates universes and begin to shed all ideas of limitation and lack.

- Where can you acknowledge and affirm abundance NOW in your life? Count your blessings. Make a gratitude list.
- Where are you experiencing lack in your life (e.g., finances, relationships, opportunities) and how can you use mental alchemy to manifest higher levels of abundance?

Law of Attraction

Like attracts like. We attract into our reality that which we are a match to vibrationally in a process called manifestation. What we manifest is an indicator of where we are in vibration and belief. The universe gives us exactly what we ask for energetically in our dominant and consistent vibrations, intentions, and beliefs. Along the path of manifesting the higher aspirations, we attract into our reality experiences that show us subconscious beliefs that are out of alignment with our desired manifestation. When we experience the manifestation of something unwanted, we can bring awareness into our subconscious beliefs and limiting patterns to upgrade our perspectives and overall vibration which creates the potential for higher manifestations within the hologram of our reality.

Our desires and emotional investments in our thoughts magnetize experiences into our reality. Earth is a dense environment filled with contrasting experiences, some wanted and some unwanted. Desire is necessary for creation, or else we would simply rest in stillness and never accomplish anything more. Some desires satisfy our false self, and some satisfy our higher calling. Some desires are from an attempt to overpower and devour, and some desires honor free will, connection, and spiritual growth. There is nothing inherently wrong with desire, yet we should grow in awareness of where that desire emerges from and the intentions behind it.

- How can you use the power of your mind to generate positive momentum towards your desired goals? Spend time visualizing and feeling the emotions of your desired outcome as if it is already received. Feel the power of this pre-matter creation and trust that the universe is assisting you in creating this outcome. Conjure your future reality in the NOW by using the power of spoken word to describe how you are bringing this dream into reality while simultaneously holding the internal image of it already manifested.

Law of Resonance

Everything within an environment entrains to and evolves toward the dominant vibration. Every person has various vibrations happening simultaneously within their experience. While we may have a vibration of love in our hearts, we may also have a vibration of fear that reduces our overall vibrational frequency. If we want to be in a higher vibration, it is vital that we clear and reconcile our lower vibrations to align with wholeness, joy, and freedom.

The power behind manifestation is subtle energy and vibration. As we grow on our path of mastery, we become powerful deliberate creators. The Law of Resonance shows that we can transform our lower energies so that our dominant vibration is high in frequency and aligned with Love and Wisdom. The Law of Attraction draws into our reality that which we are a match to so that we can understand our vibrational output and do the work to raise in vibration.

Those who deny the existence of their shadow and try to be "positive vibes only" spiritually bypass their suffering. This only perpetuates more experiences of suffering because they still hold lower vibrational attitudes in their subconscious. When someone decides to consciously do "shadow work," they can refine their overall vibration and manifest more of what they truly desire in a faster process. This path may seem more painful, but it requires less effort over time and eliminates unnecessarily prolonged cycles of suffering. Illuminated Quantum Healing makes shadow work easy to do, enjoyable, and even one session can process a lot of the self-defeating patterns that cause suffering and illness.

Law of Compensation/Reciprocity

What you give, you get back. What you sow, you reap. What goes around comes around. What is important here is if the action is born from love or fear. What you give in love with the vibration of abundance comes back as love from the universe, possibly through another person, place, or experience. What you give out in fear, doubt, and scarcity will always come back as a reflection of that energy. In karma yoga, the path of service and altruistic action, everything is to be done in service of life without expectations of reward. You simply perform an action with love in your heart for the sake of doing it, not because it somehow benefits you now or in the future. That being said, selfless service is one of the best ways to cancel negative karma.

- Are there areas in your life where you are primarily acting for self-serving benefit where you can instead take the approach of selfless service and altruistic action?

Law of Action

This law describes how we must act on our dreams and desires to bring them into reality. Newton's First Law of Motion relates to inertia and states that an object will stay at rest or in motion until it is influenced by another force. Your input is essential for you to get what you want from your life. To manifest our higher aspirations, we can apply consistent intention, thought, speech, and action in the direction of that aspiration. Nothing changes if nothing changes, and we are the creators of change in our reality.

Newton's Second Law of Motion relates to momentum and states that acceleration is parallel and directly proportional to force. The more you consistently practice a new way of thinking, feeling, and acting, the more momentum you pick up and the faster that change will happen. You can further accelerate your growth by being surrounded by a community of those who are excited about and interested in your growth.

- Where can you grow in disciplined focus and consistency to achieve your goals and manifest your dreams?
- What are your gifts, talents and strengths? How can you use them more dynamically in your life to manifest your highest destiny and serve the greater good?

As we practice acknowledging and applying these Laws of the Universe, we begin to form our life into a higher expression. We can step out of mundane biological evolution and endless karmic cycles and live in a world of magic and alchemy. We can become conscious extensions of Universal Law and evolve out of the ordinary into the extraordinary. We can use the Universal Laws to unshackle ourselves from creations born from habit into a visionary path of artistry and deliberate creation.

SEVEN

Ascension and Descension Cycles of Consciousness

All of life is in a constant state of evolution. Forms come into existence for some time and then they evolve into something different. Nothing is static. Within this dynamic flow of evolution and devolution exists patterns and cycles of change, evolutionary rhythms that guide manifestation in an eternal dance. Imagine the gears of the clock with many different timings of revolutions all contributing to the grand turning of time. Each segment of time is a container for certain processes to occur that affect the All. Let us look at the cycles of change on the planet and how human consciousness evolves through these interrelated time cycles.

Day and Night

Gaia, our beloved planet Earth, spins around its axis, creating our perception of day and night. We have limited hours of daylight during this creation cycle to activate our intentions and work towards our goals. As day fades into night, we begin to unwind and prepare for sleep so we can rejuvenate for our next segment of creation. Each day is a new beginning on our path of learning and expansion.

Four Seasons of the Year

Earth spins around the Sun creating the seasons of spring, summer, autumn, and winter. We can see this as one giant breath cycle of the Earth as life explodes into growth and slowly fades into stages of hibernation and decomposition before beginning the cycle all over again.

Spring in one hemisphere is like the Earth's inhale as life bursts into creative flow as the Earth's surface is warmed by the Sun and the hours of the day grow longer. Seeds are planted, and inspiration gives birth to new creative projects and ventures.

During the summer segment, we tend to the seeds we have sown and use the fire of the long summer days to put consistent action into our creations. This is a time of exploration and community as everyone comes into the Sun for fun and creative play.

We finalize our creative projects during the autumn segment and begin to harvest the fruits of our labor in preparation for winter. This is a perfect time to trim back the decaying parts of ourselves that inhibit our creative process.

As winter approaches and daylight hours shorten, we retreat inward for contemplation and meditation. This is a perfect time for dreaming and visioning what we want to create in our next journey around the Sun.

The Great Year: Precession of the Equinoxes

The Precession of the Equinoxes, or the axial precession, is the third movement of the Earth. It travels with our solar system around a Central Sun, commonly thought to be Alcyone in the constellation of seven stars commonly known as the Pleiades.

Different cultures and groups have different ways of measuring the Precession of the Equinoxes. It is commonly agreed that this cycle takes approximately 26,000 years. As the Earth moves around this spiral, the Earth's north and south celestial poles seem to make circles against the darkness of space as the spheroid shape of the Earth is pulled on by the magnetic force of the Sun, causing a "wobble" in our rotation. Moving just like a giant gyroscope, this wobble slowly changes our seasons' timing and the alignment of the Earth with a North Star. Our North Star changes during the wobble, alternating between Vega and Polaris in cycles of 13,000 years. Earth is currently aligned with Polaris, but it will align with Vega in the constellation of Lyra in the future.

The Precession of the Equinoxes is segmented and measured by the Sun's timing during the Vernal Equinox in the Northern Hemisphere as the Sun seemingly travels backward through the 12 zodiac constellations. Within the Great Year, each astrological age or Great Month, rises and falls in a timeframe that lasts approximately 2,166 years.

The 26,000-year cycle can be looked at as 13,000 years of waking up, called Ascension, and 13,000 years of falling asleep in consciousness, called

Descension. The Sanskrit traditions segment the Great Year into four eras called yugas, which describe the Golden Ages of Consciousness (*Satya Yuga*), where perfect Unity and Divine Paradise exist on the Earth. These Golden Ages slowly begin to erode as humanity's consciousness begins to deepen into sleep (*Treta* and *Dvapara Yugas*). War and pestilence begin to cover the Earth, and shadow invades humanity's heart and consciousness. Disease and degradation devolve us until we reach the apex of a Dark Age of Consciousness (*Kali Yuga*). Slowly, the spiritual sun begins to rise in humanity's hearts as consciousness begins to wake up and remember its divinity as humanity ascends through the Dvapara and Treta Yugas to shine in the full glory of the Age of Truth, the Satya Yuga.

Dark Ages and Descension Cycles

Ascension leader Gigi Young made a wonderful video summarizing the shifting of astrological ages that inspired these next summaries. She has a wonderful way of describing esoteric knowledge in a simple way.

During the descension cycles, darkness and distortion begin to infiltrate human consciousness as we move into The Forgetting. Wisdom gives way to rational thought and, eventually, ignorance as we become completely devoid of spiritual light and higher consciousness. During this time, humanity needs to put forth great effort into spiritual growth as the veil begins to thicken and distort our perception of the Divine. During this time, our commitment to the Light is tested as we endure trials and tribulations, accruing negative karma and a "pain body" from repetitive cycles of suffering and delusion. Higher consciousness connection gives way to fear and superstition, and individual spirituality becomes dogmatic religion as we forget our True Nature and believe God to be outside of ourselves.

In descension cycles, times of The Forgetting, we see an increase in the shadow of our consciousness as the exalted masculine and feminine parts of our consciousness begin to decay from the absence of spiritual light. The Divine Masculine energy begins to distort and overpower the Divine Feminine. The Goddess and Divine Feminine archetypes lose their value, and the Godhead is typically seen as male. Emotions and intuition lose importance to analytical thinking and science as humanity moves from the unity of the heart to the duality of the mind. The feminine energy in men and women is repressed and oppressed. Disease, famine, and war begin to spread across the Earth as our collective inner world is outpictured in Earth's reality. As the world darkens spiritually, nobility decays into political corruption as unity crumbles into domination and trickery.

During these times, spiritual truth is only taught to the elect, and many noble people dedicate their lives to protecting the Divine Feminine in all forms during these dark times. We can look to the most recent Dark Ages to see the burning of sacred books, the witch trials, slavery, and even God being externalized and personified as a vengeful, jealous man who destroys those who do not obey him. It is during these times that advanced spiritual beings from the higher realms incarnate to protect the sacred teachings as humanity moves through these times of density.

Golden Ages and Ascension Cycles

At the end of the Dark Ages, the spiritual light begins to build as we begin to remember our divinity, and the transformative power of ascension begins to awaken in our hearts and consciousness once more.

During ascension cycles, we see a rise in the Divine Feminine within humanity. Spirituality heightens as people begin to connect with the Divine through the development and resurgence of ritual and spiritual practices. The veil thins between the physical and spiritual realms, and we can access Spirit with increasing ease. Healing practices are cultivated and shared to heal the karmas and disease developed through our unconscious conditioning and habits during the Dark Ages.

Ascension cycles move us towards a matriarchal society where we begin to acknowledge the Feminine Aspect of Source, the Goddess, the Holy Spirit. It is at this time that we see a softening in the masculine energies, and the feminine energies begin to rise in the consciousness of humanity as we remember our purity and divine identity. On the New Earth, we will live in balance with the exalted expressions and union of Divine Masculine and Divine Feminine working together towards higher and higher harmony.

Matriarchal societies highly value emotions and intuition, and spirituality tends to focus more on cycles of the Moon and the fertility of nature because we see ourselves as part of the cosmic and Earth rhythms. This is a time of nurturing and the return of "white magic" that inspires harmony and unity. Women begin to find their voices and fill positions of leadership, leading humanity back to their hearts. Men become more compassionate and noble. Spiritual light begins to pervade humanity's consciousness. The Divine Masculine begins to heal and return to balance, and all gender expressions begin to walk together towards common goals of peace and balance.

During these high times, creativity and sensuality flourish as we tune into our creative, divine power. This is a time of discovery as we release the Dark Ages' shadows and move into higher experiences of radiant glory and opulence.

Astrological Ages

Each ascension and descension phase takes on the qualities of the zodiac sign that Earth and our Sun align with during the Spring Equinox in the Northern Hemisphere. We can look at the high points and low points of society during various periods of civilizations to understand what astrological age we were in at that time.

The birthing of each new astrological age challenges the practices and beliefs of the previous age. Each transition tests our ability to adapt to the shifting tide. This is when the "wheat is separated from the chaff" as revolutions and uprisings emerge from the shift in consciousness, and old ideas are tested by visionary thoughts of the dawning of the new astrological age.

We have been in an ascension phase for some time now and are shifting out of the Age of Pisces symbolized by the symbol of the fish connected to Christ Jesus's life and into the Age of Aquarius, the beginning of our next Golden Age as the redemptive power of the Holy Spirit is dispensed throughout the Earth to return Earth and humanity to the original divine blueprint.

The Age of Aquarius

The sign of Aquarius is the sign of the Water Bearer pouring consciousness and life-giving water onto Earth's soil. As we shift into the Aquarian Age, we are starting to see a rise in humanitarian efforts as we begin to think globally and holistically. We see a rise in visionary and futuristic creations as our imaginations burst with creativity. There is a deep drive for transformation as humanity rejects ideas of limitation and control. We are becoming independent and empowered creators, rebellious against the stagnant and controlling ways of the past. We are beginning to see rapid technological progress on Earth and a growing desire to travel amongst the stars. There is a strengthening of inner discipline as we begin to actualize our visionary dreams and ideals by refining and unifying our body, mind, and inner Source.

During this time, we should question everything we have believed to be true. While the expansion of ascension can be exhilarating, we need to exercise prudence to discern what beliefs and societal structures truly support our highest aspirations as individuals and as collectives. As we transition out of the Piscean Age and into the Age of Aquarius, many shadows will come up into our conscious awareness that have been hidden in our individual and collective unconscious memory. This will coincide with the revealing of the efforts by the negatively polarized groups and individuals who wish to keep humanity from awakening to our True Nature. There will come a time where these control systems will no longer be able to work their dark magic on humanity's consciousness and full disclosure will occur. Humanity will see how we have been kept in the dark of ignorance by the controlling elite cabal systems and from there, we will create a New Earth with true freedom for all!

Photon Belt

Another influence over planetary ascension is what is called the Photon Belt. It has been mentioned a few times in sessions, but I have not yet asked many questions specific to it. I will give a brief summary of my understanding of it based on the research I have done online, comparing it to what has been said in sessions.

The Photon Belt is said to be a band of radiation encircling the Pleiades. As our solar system travels around Alcyone, it intersects this band of light two times. The last time the Earth crossed the Photon Belt would have been in the times of the ancient lost culture of Atlantis approximately 13,000 years ago. When we pass through the belt, all distortion is brought to the surface to be purified by the Light. It takes approximately 2,000 years to journey through this multidimensional light field. Crossing the threshold is an initiation to see if we are ready to release all our shadows and ascend to the next level of experience. In Atlantis, we did not make the mark which caused us to implode on our own consciousness. Humanity still wanted to "play God" and live out of integrity. So, humanity had to start our consciousness development all over again. More of this is discussed later in this book.

We started traveling through this band of light around 2012 and will continue through it for the next 2,000 years. Every shadow will be purified and the "wheat will be separated from the chaff" as only those who can raise their frequency will continue with their current physical life. I have been assured many times that humanity and the Earth WILL make it this time and that the Earth will ascend into her Fourth Density form taking with her all who have aligned with this ascension pathway through the love and openness in their hearts. Truly, humanity's heart is currently being weighed against the Feather of Truth!

The Age of Aquarius ushers in the beginning of our next ascent into the Golden Era, and it comes with many challenges as we are forced to choose between adaptation or decay. Each of us gets to choose between truth and divinity's upward spiral or to continue down the death spiral of entropy and ignorance. Not a single person on this planet is insignificant, as we all play our role in contributing to our collective future. No one knows the exact details and chain of events that lay ahead of us, and probabilities and timelines of events are constantly in flux. It is up to each of us to ignite the fire of our inner Source and walk through this collapsing paradigm into the next Golden Age of Gaia.

Other cycles exist beyond the Precession of the Equinoxes as infinite alignments and patterns play out as the myriad of galaxies, stars, and planets spiral around the Great Central Sun of this universe. As humanity moves into the Age of Aquarius, we are about to complete a much larger cycle that culminates with a Grand Reset of Life on planet Earth via the Great Solar Flash. Humanity is about to take a quantum leap in consciousness and rapidly ascend to the greatness seen in the glorious Golden Age of Lemuria, the purest high-consciousness civilization that existed upon the Earth.

All karma must and will be balanced as we manifest New Earth and become a People of Light!

EIGHT
Ascension Symptom Care

Lightbody ascension practices are found in many ancient cultures, especially in India, Tibet, and Ancient Egypt. The systems focus on transformation by refining the physical, vital, emotional, mental, intuitional, intellectual, and spiritual bodies so that a being embodies Divine Light and their Divine I AM Presence. As we clear our lower energies, we make way for the Light of the Higher Realms to descend into our physical vessel so that we radiate Light and Truth out into the world.

In the past, once an initiate reached a high enough vibration and the highest level of enlightenment they could reach in the body, they would consciously shed the body to continue learning in the higher realms in their Lightbody. Sometimes they would go into a trance and consciously leave the body, or some highly advanced initiates who could control the frequency of their cells would spin them faster and faster until they shifted beyond the visible light spectrum into the higher realms as their physical body dissolved into thin air. Yeshua ben Joseph (Jesus) made this ascension process popular, but it has also been documented and written about by other cultures, especially the Egyptians and Tibetan Buddhists.

What is different about our upcoming ascension is that we will be transforming our physical body into a lighter form and taking it with us into the next dimension of consciousness and reality. What was once only available to select initiates through arduous purification and healing practices in secluded temples and monasteries is now available to all people committed to compassionate heart-based living and have done the work to raise their overall vibration.

As we prepare for Gaia's transformation from Third Density Earth to Fourth Density Gaia, our DNA is being restored back to the Adamic form, the original pristine human Lightbody. Many alterations have been made to the human DNA throughout humanity's time on Earth, and we are in a purging process of all the distortions stored within our multidimensional genetic structure and sequencing.

These distortions are the product of genetic implantation from other star races, ancestral memory, mental fields absorbed from the collective thought patterns, toxicity from our environments, damage from the cataclysm of Atlantis, and more. As these ascension energies move through our system, they clear any blockages we have accrued so that we can hold more light. This can appear as cold/flu-like symptoms, increased body heat, heightened intuition, foggy mind, dizziness, chest pain, digestive issues, vivid dreams, emotional purging, paranormal experiences, ringing in the ears, dehydration, and more.

Below is a list of guidelines to support the ascension and Lightbody activation and recalibration processes. This is not meant to be "medical advice" but speaks to common experiences held by myself and others in the global ascension community.

If you feel that you are unhealthy and at risk for serious health concerns, please see a medical professional. I highly recommend seeing a medical professional who treats clients holistically. Western medicine is trained to focus on symptoms. Eastern medicine and holistic healthcare professionals are trained to look for root causes and treat entire systems to bring the body back into homeostasis.

Meditation: Calling in Light

Meditation is a crucial step in this process. Developing self-awareness helps you discern what is best for your path so that you can release what no longer serves you. Meditation practices that utilize conscious breathing are some of the best tools to ground your energy, clear out stagnant energy, and revitalize your personal energy field as fresh life force enters through the breath. Visualizing clear, bright light moving through the body helps raise the body's vibration and transform dense energy into a more refined and clear energy signature. Let the sunshine in!

Dehydration

Many health problems stem from chronic dehydration. Drink plenty of fresh spring water to hydrate the tissues and cells of the body. Municipal water sources often contain chlorine, fluoride, or other chemicals that poison our bodies and mind. Adding trace-mineral hydration salts to your water helps the water absorb into the cells. Also, consider taking a "cell salt" supplement to support healthy cellular function. Adding magnesium to your hydration practice will also help with discomfort in the chest/heart region when assimilating the energies. This will also help with headaches and anxious feelings.

Silica Supplements

It has been recommended that we all take silica supplements to support our body's transition from being carbon-based to a crystalline, silica-based Lightbody. This will help with achy joints, cognitive functioning, and more.

Essential Oils and Plant Medicine

Nature knows best. Herbs and plant extracts work with our body's cells and consciousness to bring our systems into homeostasis. This includes medicines like psylocibin, cannabis, hemp, kava, and other plant allies to help us soothe the ascension process and connect with higher intelligence for healing and transformation. Of course, intention and safety are important for all medicine journeys. Keep it sacred!

High-quality essential oils that are certified pure and organic safely work with the body's cells to support the body's natural ability to heal itself. Some oils can be taken internally, and most are safe for topical and aromatic use. Check with each oil's health and protocol guidelines to understand how to use the oil safely and properly.

When using topically, consider using a vegetable/nut-based carrier oil to help spread the essential oil across the skin. If an essential oil is applied topically and causes irritation, dilute and clean with a carrier oil. Do not use water as this drives the essential oil further into the tissue.

Detoxify the Body

Physical symptoms include a variety of detoxification symptoms as toxins are released from the body. You may notice a diet change as the body craves fresh, organic fruits and vegetables and less meat. There will not be meat or killing of any kind when we shift to the New Earth consciousness.

Everyone should follow their own guidance about what nourishment their body needs at any given time. Periodic fasting can help the elimination process as well as eating a naturally detoxifying diet. Eating fresh greens fills the body systems with biophotons, light particles to support healthy system functionality. Switch to natural, organic products versus products with toxic chemical ingredients to reduce your organs' toxic load. You may feel guided to do a cleanse regimen like a liver cleanse or kidney cleanse, or a heavy metal detox to help the body eliminate toxins.

Cellular Oxidation

Radiation from cosmic energies, solar events, 5G radiation, and other energies puts stress on our body's cells. Increase antioxidant intake and supplements that promote cellular health and reverse the effects of oxidative stress.

Alkalize the Body

Reduce the body's acidity to reduce inflammation and support the body's natural ability to heal itself. This includes eating a mostly "sattvic" diet or a "yogic diet" which is simple and free from processed ingredients and synthetics. Practices like drinking apple cider vinegar, fresh lemon juice, or citrus essential oils help to break apart and eliminate toxic build-up in the body.

Detoxify People, Places, and Things

Spend less and less time around people that are vexatious to your system. Find like-minded people who are loving and gentle to spend your time with. Avoid places with highly charged energies when you are feeling extra sensitive. Many find that they need to spend more quality time alone or with their pets and limit their social interactions to focus on their own healing and expansion. Declutter your home to free up stagnant energy. As within, so without!

Rest and Sleep

Listen to the body and honor when it is asking for rest. At times, the body will need much more rest and sleep as it adjusts to the shifting frequencies. Sometimes, you may not be able to sleep because of the rush of plasma entering your field from the ascension energies. Be gentle with yourself. Natural sleep aids, teas, and herbal supplements help the body stay in deeper sleep to feel refreshed when you awaken. Chamomile and lavender can help you prepare for a deep night's rest.

Get Into Nature

Nature has a grounding and centering effect on our consciousness and nervous system. Take frequent trips into nature away from people, pollution, and technology. "Earthing" or walking barefoot on the ground helps to ground pent-up energy in your nervous system, leaving you feeling grounded and clear. If you cannot stand on soil, you can stand on a layer of sea salt to ground your energy. Use a container to stand in so that you do not make a mess!

Ringing in the Ears

The electromagnetic fields of the Earth and the planetary grid will be unstable in the process, as will our own energetic field. The ringing of the ears is common for people at different times as waves of plasma enter the Earth. Some people find themselves to be extra sensitive to Electromagnetic Frequencies (EMFs). Many devices and crystals (e.g., shungite) are available to help reduce the negative effects of EMFs on the body and consciousness. It is suggested that we take as much time as we can to get off our devices, out of range of Wi-Fi and cell towers, and immerse ourselves in the regenerative field of Nature. Return to the wild and wonderful!

Headaches, Dizziness, and Cognitive Functioning

These energies affect our minds as we shed lower beliefs and upgrade the brain's anatomy and cognitive functioning. This could manifest as states of confusion and feeling sensations in the brain, including headaches, energy movement, and pulsations.

Dizziness and headaches can be a sign that you need more water and need to ground excess energy. Consciously ground the energy through intention and meditative practices or walk barefoot on the earth. Increase water intake and rest until the dizziness subsides. Add hydration salts, trace minerals, cellular salts, and silica supplements to support the process. Essential oils like peppermint and lavender help soothe head and neck tension to alleviate pressure in the head.

Digestive System Issues

The digestive system not only processes food to create energy, but the solar plexus digests subtle energy for a variety of processes. Many find that their digestive system is either over or underactive at different times. I recommend using a natural digestive supplement, digestive enzyme supplement, or laying of hands to support the healing process. Essential oils like ginger and peppermint help support healthy digestive processes.

Low Energy and Fatigue

Sometimes, no matter how much you rest, it may not feel like enough. Using invigorating essential oils can boost the mood and increase focus. There are many natural food supplements to use to boost energy like cacao, maca, and spirulina. If you use caffeine, I suggest using tea, especially yerba mate, versus coffee to reduce acidity in the body. Essential oils like peppermint and citrus oils help to lift the mood and focus the mind.

Soaking in Water

Water is a powerful tool to use to ground and clear energy. Find natural sources of water to swim in or soak your feet. Take baths with natural salts and minerals added to the water to help clear and restore. Adding your favorite essential oils, candles, and soft music or recorded meditations helps amplify the bath's healing effects. Frequent showers also help to reinvigorate the senses and clear your personal energy.

Emotional Triggering and Heart Activation

Collective, ancestral, and individual trauma stored within the body's systems and DNA are being reactivated and cleared. Many experience this as a deep churning in the heart, fatigue, vivid dreams, and more. Aromatherapy is one of the quickest natural ways to soothe emotions.

Increased Intuitive Abilities

Intuition, psychic gifts, and multidimensional awareness are increasing rapidly as our lower energies clear out of the chakra and subtle energy systems, creating an expanded empathetic nervous system. To avoid unnecessary suffering and psychic attack, one can cultivate a strong and clear subtle energy system and grow in heart-centered discernment and energetic hygiene.

Vivid and Prophetic Dreams

Many are experiencing vivid dreams as their subconscious works out limiting beliefs and unprocessed trauma in their dreamtime. Some dreams are teaching dreams where people experience themselves in learning environments practicing new skills. Some are healing dreams where people report miraculous, rapid healing often conducted by extraterrestrial beings or higher light beings. Some people are reporting meetings with other souls in their soul group, where Ascension topics are discussed. Some people are reporting that they are being brought aboard spacecraft and introduced to galactic beings and receive updated intel on Earth changes and Ascension information.

Some people do not have any dream recall during the ascension process because the information being discussed in the dreams would keep them from playing out the role they need to in their regular human life. Some people have even traveled to the New Earth or future timelines where they get to experience life after humanity and Earth have ascended.

Each person is different in how they handle this process. Do not judge yourself based on how others are handling it. Also, one minute you can be fine, and the next minute have an emotional purge and a headache. Let the process happen. Make a practice of nourishing yourself.

This process can be intense, but it comes with great benefits! Thank you for facing your shadow and aligning with Truth, Knowledge, and Wisdom. You are so brave!

NINE

Shifting to New Earth

We are now at the final moments before this Grand Shift. From a higher perspective, we are being divided between positive polarity collectives and negative polarity collectives. This means that some are awakening to a higher love within, and others are maintaining a duality-based consciousness and will continue a downward spiral of entropy and destruction, eventually exiting the planet through physical death.

Over the coming years, people will be moving on the planet to the places they have decided to be for these final events leading up to the Main Event Horizon and shift in consciousness. Those who are awakening are beginning to find others who are awakening. Much of this has been happening on the internet, and more and more events and gatherings will be happening across the world as people come together in One Heart. What a cause for celebration as we all begin to see the familiar Light in one another's eyes and awaken to the game we have been playing with ourselves since the beginning of time.

Not everyone is meant to continue with Earth and ascending humanity into this next Age of Light. Their souls will continue their maturation process in other incarnations on other planets where the Third Dimension exists or whatever dimension best serves their growth. Some of these embodied souls are seen as the "villains" and "traitors" that will catalyze and amplify the desire to awaken in the hearts and minds of those who are choosing Love, Light, Unity, and Harmony. The villain archetype is crucial for Ascension. We see this character in Set from Egypt for the resurrection of Osiris and in Judas for the ascension process of Jesus. Each awakening soul is invited to play the role of Collective Messiahship and share the good news of Ascension and the Higher Mysteries so that those who hunger for Truth can be set free from the entropic thought patterns of service-to-self, ancestral trauma, and negative karma.

It is wise to remember that "everything is not what it seems" in this school of illusion. Everything is happening for a Divine Purpose. We are invited to stand as pillars of Unconditional Love and broadcast the messages of New Earth. For those who have ears to listen, let them hear the "good news" of what is to come. Let us all reveal the thought processes and beliefs that have created our own inner tyrant and an inner adversary so that we no longer need to see it outpictured in our reality. Let us choose peace. Let us choose harmony. Let us choose unity. Let us choose Ascension!

Prophecy

Anyone who does intuitive readings can tell you that their prophecies and intuitive understandings are based on energy at that particular moment of the vision or reading. Free will gives us the ability to choose a higher timeline by releasing density and making higher choices. With so many volunteers and support from galactic beings and the higher realms, we have moved beyond much of the death and destruction that has been foretold by prophets and seers of the past. Even modern prophecies are subject to change as we are constantly shifting between probabilities of how this will all play out.

Every action you as an individual or we as a collective make shifts us into different timeline potentials for the unfolding of The Event. Our job is to maintain the highest vibration and the highest vision for the highest potential outcome so that we can guide our collective experience into a more harmonious unfolding. The power is in our hands, minds, and hearts. We can come together as a collective and use the power of focused attention and loving intention to guide us all into peace and unity. The power and potency of positive and empowering prayer holds the keys to manifesting our most desired outcomes. While some cataclysmic events are necessary for this shift to occur, we can avoid unnecessary suffering by coming together in unified prayer. Together, we can create a powerful prayer field to influence weather patterns, seismic activity, and harmonize collective emotional experiences to avoid events that could cause massive suffering and transition to a higher timeline of experience.

There will be those that will stay focused on the doom and gloom narrative that is widely accepted and propagated by world religions. By focusing on the darkness and suffering, they will likely create that experience for themselves on their personal timeline. We, as the human collective, do have the ability to collapse timelines that no longer serve us. We have a choice. It is the same choice that there has always been — between unconditional love and surrender to the Divine Plan or else live in fear, judgment, and inner turmoil. Even when chaotic events are happening around the world, it is up to us to hold the highest outcome in our vision and be unwavering in our ability to hold the Light.

Discernment and False Teachers

Discernment is of the utmost importance at this time. When the energies are high, so are the emotions. Many wild and misleading ideas will be shared amongst the collective. It is up to each individual to grow in the power of discernment to feel what resonates as Truth within them. If a message generates fear or panic within you, walk away from that material. Many religious leaders, government officials, and spiritual teachers will have their shadows brought into the light where they have abused their power, especially those who have claimed to be the voice of God. This includes the ascension community! It is important not to put any human on a pedestal. We are all subject to shadow. Instead, place your faith in your Inner Light and the unfolding of the higher evolutionary plan. For the most part, I have stopped listening to most spiritual teachers and have instead invested time learning to listen to my own internal guidance and the study of sacred texts to grow in my own spiritual capacity. Follow your heart. It knows the way. The mechanics of discernment are taught later in this book in the section about the *vijnanamaya kosha*, the Intellectual Wisdom Body.

Many Are Exiting the Earth School

Once a soul has aligned with an exit plan, no outside force can stop it from exiting. Many people will leave their bodies during these events per their design before entering this life. Every contract has to play out, and a balance must be achieved. As these souls go through their physical death experience, they will support us from the "other side." Another reason people die is that they take their fear and karma out of the Earth realm, which increases the collective vibration of Earth.

As the shadow systems and shadow players are revealed to the masses, many will have to face the fact that they have supported these systems unknowingly and in doing so have supported systems that have killed countless people. I was told that when the truth comes out about the cancer industry, many will be outraged because of all the loved ones they lost from cancer and other illnesses that could have been saved if the controllers had not created the conditions that cause cancer and repressed the healing technologies and medicines. Many people will have to face the fact that they ridiculed us "new agers" and "conspiracy theorists" who were right all along. Disclosure of the shadow system will cause people to have heart attacks from a broken heart; people will kill one another in rage; many will commit suicide or die from psychosis because they cannot live with the truth.

Some people will not be able to hold the vibration of these high energies and die suddenly or quickly decline in health because they have not shed dense energies and will not evolve. Some souls decided they would leave the Earth School as a group, possibly in a natural disaster or casualty of violence. During these times, we will need one another to support each other through the natural grieving processes. This is another reason why we need more people with a higher perspective of death and the afterlife, as many will be looking for answers.

Not everyone is meant to ascend into the New Earth. Some are meant to have simple lives and exit this world for the next journey throughout the cosmos. Ascension involves reconciling judgment within us for those who seem not to be "waking up" or seem to be following the false narrative presented by the controllers. They are offering us an opportunity to release polarized perspectives and be open to nondual understanding. Even the most "evil" people are offering us bitter medicine to grow into deeper compassion and clarity. This does not mean that we condone the actions that cause harm, it just means that we do not have to hold hatred, judgment, or contempt towards them. Every single being here on the planet is serving this great awakening whether they are conscious of it or not. All is Source; all is the One Being experiencing itself in myriad forms and polarities for the purpose of truly "knowing thy Self."

Much grief will sweep through humanity during these next stages. They are the most difficult to bear and many will experience intense grief. Grief is a powerful emotion. It carves deep into the heart and seems to stay around for eternity for some. We can use the power of High Alchemy to use grief as a powerful tool for transformation. I invite us all to use the pain of what is to come to launch us into our sovereign power to reform our reality. Use it to become a voice for the Earth and for those who have suffered under the tyranny of these shadow systems. All of this ends when humanity stands in its power and says ENOUGH!

Rapture

This is a complex multidimensional topic because I have only heard of this a few times. This type of event is not connected to any religion. Since it is a common question, I will share what I have learned through my sessions.

The first point to share is that there will not be a mass disappearance of bodies as depicted in some modern Christian interpretations. The main way of departure will be from people leaving their bodies through physical death as they finish their contracts. This is not a judgment. It is simply part of the plan as they have only agreed to live through so much of the process.

One other type of departure I have heard of, but only once, is the departure of some starseeds. I have heard of two major departures from the planet for souls from other star systems who volunteered to incarnate on Earth as humans to assist in the Great Awakening. Some starseeds are only on the planet to help energetically until a tipping point occurs in our collective consciousness. Once that marker is reached, one large group of people will be taken from the planet, followed by another group a few months later. I have been told that there are twelve "New Earths" including this one that we are all currently on. Each of these planets will be home to different humans and life forms. I do not know much about the other planets as much of my sessions have been focused on the shift of Gaia/Terra from the Third Density to the Fourth, aka the Fifth Dimension. From my understanding, there will be considerably fewer people living on the planet once it finalizes its shift.

In my second meeting with the Council of 24 Elders, I was shown how I would have the capacity to jump between realities or embodiments. It seemed as though I would be able to be in one embodiment in 5D New Earth and then "flip myself inside out" to be in the 3D Earth reality to assist in some way as if I would be living in both realities simultaneously. I still do not completely understand what was shown to me, but I thought I would write about it in case it is helpful for someone. Part of the intention with this book is to have the book printed in physical form so that it would be available for people if timelines split into different experiences of The Event.

It is common for people to question if they are going to "make it." This question is rooted in fear and insecurity and deserves time for reflection and healing so that you can embody the higher love of your Divine Nature. No one is "left behind" which means that you are exactly where you need to be, and Source is with you always. Trust in the process and stay present in your heart.

Potential Timelines of War

As part of the design, service-to-self forces will likely destroy one another as they war against each other to control the planet. War, battles, protests, revolts, riots, and other such events are likely to happen as we get closer to the launch point of the main event — the pulse of Light from our Sun via the Great Central Sun.

This experience of war is for those who agreed to such an experience before incarnating. There will be places of peace and places of conflict. Those who exit the Earth School are simply done with their life contract and will continue to their next incarnation in whatever level of spiritual growth is appropriate for them. The wars and destruction serve as a contrast for those who are awakening to anchor us into knowing that Love and Peace are truly The Way.

True and lasting peace, the Heaven on Earth reality is not possible in the third dimension. This true peace and harmony are found in the fifth-dimensional consciousness. Until then, conflict and duality remain as karmic contracts play out before 5D consciousness fully manifests across the remnant of humanity upon 5D Earth.

My understanding is that there are a few different groups of service-to-self consciousness that are fighting for control of the planet and humanity. The overlord structures coordinate events to create a crisis and suffering and then offer a solution to manipulate people to follow their agenda (problem-reaction-solution). This bait-and-hook method of mind control hijacks the goodwill intentions and actions of the unaware who unknowingly follow the mainstream narrative because they feel that they are helping the situation. Coordinated power outages, food and supply shortages, and other false flag events are planned to create fear in humanity. Those who are connected to their inner truth and higher consciousness connection will be able to see these events for what they truly are, while others will not as they are still under the spell.

This dark initiative is powered through psychological manipulation tactics used through subliminal messaging and suggestion using the trance-induced state created by watching a television or screened device. Phrases are repeated by global leaders, politicians, and other influential people to implant the overlord-approved narrative into the listeners' consciousness which subconsciously programs them to follow the nefarious agenda. The war on consciousness and the battle for dominion over Planet Earth and humanity is real and we are watching it play out in real time.

Collapsing of the Old Systems

All of society's systems are being forced to shift with this energy or crumble to make way for the new. Governments, financial institutions, religious institutions, judicial systems, educational systems, and so on have been used to keep humanity in the lower consciousness and enslaved through various methods. All of these systems will be reconciled over the next years. This is especially true of the collapse of the financial systems which must dissolve so that the Cabal-run control systems that depend on currency to fund their dark projects will run out of financial backing. Humanity will no longer "chase the dollar" to create their worth or security and will instead realize their inherent worth and source all that they need from the quantum field and Gaia.

Governing systems will shift towards councils of representatives who will be selected based on spiritual resonance. In the New Earth, everyone will perform the role that is most in alignment with their soul's path. No more slave jobs! The old system of economics will give way to a quantum-based financial system.

Earth Changes

Parallel to our ascension symptoms, Gaia is going through her own clearing process before she shifts into her higher, lighter form. Volunteers on the surface and galactic beings have been assisting this transition by helping Gaia transmute some of the dense energy built up over millions of years. Seismic and volcanic activity, massive storms, and abnormal weather patterns are likely to increase as the planet's energies and toxic areas are cleansed. This is like a cat or a dog that shakes and shimmies after it gets injured. This natural movement is mirrored by the Earth as Gaia releases her pent-up energy.

Gaia is a powerful and sovereign being. She permits humanity to live upon her and go through the karmic lessons necessary to remember our higher consciousness identity and unity with All. What we see happening with the Earth in terms of climate change is a reflection of the imbalance within us. She is incredibly patient with us. She could shake us all off in a heartbeat if she wanted to! The Controllers have been using the "save the Earth" narrative to convince us to give up our freedoms and to pay more money to fill their bank accounts. If we truly want the Earth to be clean and clear, it is the global elite control systems that need to be dissolved so that the land can be freed up. It is the greed born from service-to-self consciousness that needs to be eradicated. I imagine that the Controllers will use the Earth changes to further their narrative but those who know, who are connected to Spirit and our Earth Mother, will know what is truly occurring.

Crustal shifts, pole shifts, and water displacement will reorient the planet's surface as has happened in previous resets (Lemuria and Atlantis). This will reveal lost temples, lost technologies, and lost artifacts that will remind humanity of its galactic legacy. I was told that the Galactic Federation is working with the tectonic plates to balance the plasma of the core of the Earth to open up telepathic communication with Inner Earth civilizations such as Telos, Agartha, and other civilizations who have been keeping ancient records and protecting advanced technologies from the times of Lemuria and Atlantis specifically for these times. While many humans have already been communicating with Inner Earth beings, physical meetings will begin soon.

I have heard of many big fires around the world as well. I share this information cautiously because I know that we can create the future that we want. It all comes down to the collective consciousness intention and what we have agreed to in our soul contracts before incarnating. Again, I have been told that much of the destruction has been averted already and that Earth changes will not be as severe as once prophesied.

This is a natural process, and there is nothing to fear. You are always where you need to be. If you feel safe, you are safe. If you follow fear, you have the potential to create that outcome. It is up to us to become aware of our fearful tendencies and refine them through Higher Knowledge and Faith. Trust that you are being guided to the right place for the right timing of these events.

It is wise to have some supplies available if power outages or other events occur. Having a few weeks' worth of food, water, and basic supplies can be useful if supply chains are cut off because of these shifts and changes. There are potentials for communication systems and power supplies to go down at different stages. I am told that around this time awakened people will have developed a level of telepathy that will help us communicate without the need for these systems. I am told the Earth changes will begin after the big disclosures have started and sometime after the "illusion of food shortages" and power and communication system failures created by the Cabal. One sign to watch for is the birds. I imagine that before the major Earth changes start, the migratory pathways will be disrupted for birds and other animals like whales and fish who use the electromagnetic pathways to navigate across the Earth.

Safe Havens and New Earth Communities

During this Grand Shift into the next era, safe havens will need to be organized while society goes through its transformation. Some clients speak about schools and centers of education where people will gather soon while various events and changes are happening worldwide. The centers will be high-vibrational environments where people can heal, connect with one another, and support others as people continue to be drawn to these vortexes. We have heard mostly about the first City of Light that will be developed in the Pacific Northwest. This community will be a place for us to create a reality that is "off to the side" from the chaos of the crumbling world. I am not sure exactly how it starts to be manifested, but I have heard that eventually this higher dimensional, etheric, crystalline city that many starseeds see in dreams and meditation will be anchored to the Earth realm. The fires in that region are clearing out the old templates held by the land and the people that need to be released to make room for the new. Many of us have this shared dream of living in healing communities because we designed this plan before we came into the Earth School. Ron and I are excited to be a part of catalyzing that collective dream and manifesting this New Earth community.

Experimental Injections

The rollout and use of the inoculations for Covid-19 are playing a significant part in the Ascension. It is an introduction of a major catalyst that will mean different things for every person, every family, every nation, and the collective story of humanity. Each of us has a unique path, and they are all part of the divine coordination of this ascension event.

In the Bible, the "End Times" prophecy speaks of the "Mark of the Beast" being implemented to control humanity. According to the prophecy, those who do not have the mark would not be able to buy or sell. This control structure sounds remarkably similar to what is happening with the inoculations for Covid-19 and the planned "Vaccine Passports" beginning to be implemented by different governments around the world. While some of the world believes the mainstream media narrative, many see this as an attempt by those in service-to-self consciousness to control and manipulate humanity. Hopefully such an experience of tyrannical control never comes to full manifestation.

The information coming through many quantum healing hypnosis sessions is that these inoculations will negatively affect the health of many people and the worldwide push for vaccination is intended to initiate humanity into another level of overlord control, moving us towards a one world tyrannical government structure. While all of the vaccines will cause issues globally, the bigger issue has to do with the negative fallout from the mRNA gene therapies. At the writing of this book, there are already global reports of myocarditis, pericarditis, rapidly growing aggressive cancers, pulmonary embolism, and sudden death. Anyone who speaks out against the Covid-19 narrative is censored, deplatformed, or silenced. I have a feeling we are just beginning to see the tip of the iceberg in terms of the long-term effects of these injections.

In my sessions, it has been described how the service-to-self forces are using the injections to broadcast low-frequency thought patterning into the injected people, causing a distortion in their minds that lowers their vibration. Something in the injections also connects the injected person to a massive Artificial Intelligence network that extends beyond this planet that tracks the people who have been injected. The signal strength of the AI technology weakens at around six months which is part of the reason for additional booster shots. It was shared that individuals have the ability to recode the AI technology and use it to broadcast light frequencies back into the AI network to assist in the dismantling of that system.

Just because someone took an injection does not necessarily mean they cannot ascend or will get sick. The human body can transmute ANYTHING! That is part of the magnificence of human design. We can overcome every entropic pattern and transform it into the highest light. Although, I certainly would not want to test that capacity on myself! Every time I have asked, there is not yet a technology on the Earth that can reverse the negative fallout, but many physical and subtle body detoxification protocols are being downloaded by lightworkers to assist in detoxification and repair. We have been told that the IQH sessions will assist with this in the future.

It is necessary to have a high light quotient and be in outstanding health and cohesion to transmute this negative technology. Detoxification protocols should be followed for the physical and subtle bodies to clear out the negative components of the injections. The people who have taken these injections must hold no resistance to the divine and clear their various bodies with whatever means necessary. If you have taken the inoculations and wish to clear them from your system, I want you to know that I believe in you and your capacity to turn this situation into something that feeds your spiritual growth and catalyzes your process of liberation. We are here to assist!

Many people have turned from the Love of Source and do not take good care of their bodies and have not awakened to the higher Light. They are going to have the most difficult job transmuting the negative effects of the inoculations and many will leave the planet.

For some people, taking the inoculation is a sign that they are still hypnotized by the narrative that is being pushed on them by the Controllers and are unawakened or just in the beginning stages of awakening. Some will take the inoculation because they have meditated on it and fully trust that this is part of their divine pathway. They are not doing it from lower ego reasons but because of divine guidance. Some will not choose to take the injections because they prefer the organic immunity of the human body and do not want to take any risk.

Now we are at the waiting and witnessing stage as we watch what these inoculations do to humanity. For some, it will be part of their exit plan from the Earth School. As I said, not everyone is meant to ascend. Some are meant to have simple lives and transition out. Many will be born in new bodies on New Earth or continue in other schools. For some, it will be a catalyst for major awakening. For planet Earth, it begins the crumbling of the "sick-for-profit" system and the rising of the people against the forces of darkness and control.

The hardest part for those taking and not taking is not to judge or go into states of fear. Even the inoculations are a test to see if we follow the *maya* into the suffering mind or if we stay in loving conscious awareness. This does not mean that we should not speak out against tyranny and injustice, yet we can let our voices be heard from a place of true empowerment and nonviolence. One who is united with their True Nature is more powerful than one thousand who are not. Together, we ARE THE WINDS OF CHANGE!

Another challenge is that during this bifurcation of consciousness, the Great Divide, most of the people that have taken the inoculations are in a different consciousness that will be difficult for ascension-focused people to be around. Our reality may be offensive to them because we are not under the spell of the mainstream narrative. It is a two-world split. We live in completely different realities side by side. The Old Earth consciousness and the New Earth consciousness occupy the Earth at the same time. I suggest finding your people, those with the Light in their eyes! Those who are on the path of seeking spiritual wisdom and spiritual knowledge. These are the ones you will build the New Earth with!

Artificial Intelligence and Microchip Implants

It is wise to exercise extreme caution when creating Artificial Intelligence as this was already an issue in our past in Atlantis. No matter how tempting, we should not allow any person or group to install microchips or AI technology on or in our human bodies. Our human body is extremely powerful, and the controlling powers will likely attempt to use these types of technology to suppress our awakening. No matter what promises are made, or conveniences may come from integrating the technology into our body, I suggest avoiding such hybridization and transhumanism while humanity still operates in 3D as hijacking is still possible and highly probable. The organic technology of our own human body is capable of telepathy, bilocation, astral travel, telekinesis, levitation, channeling higher consciousness beings, and so much more, and there is no need to give in to the allure of the promises made by Big Tech and other influential powers.

Healing

Energy medicine is the way of the future. One client described being in a safe haven community when global events were in chaos. She described a beam of light emanating from the center of the community that people who were awakening could see and travel towards to find the community. On the grounds of the community were many lightworkers with visible light emanating from their hands. She described Arcturian beings teaching advanced healing practices to humans and medical beds that rapidly heal people at the cellular level.

As the human consciousness opens, we will receive more information through channelings and hypnosis sessions like Illuminated Quantum Healing. We have tremendous amounts of information stored within our Akashic Records, our soul's memory bank. Illuminated Quantum Healing and the other quantum healing hypnosis modalities will be of great support during these next stages to help those who are ascending and to ease the suffering of those who are destined to exit the Earth realm.

Shifting to New Earth Relationships

Individuals are now finishing their karmic contracts in preparation for what is to come. Many people are finishing up karmic relationships and moving into supportive soul family relationships. Instead of the past's power and control techniques, these relationships are supportive, cooperative, and empower individuals to be their own Sovereign Self. Many are reporting that they have left the patterns of karmic romantic relationships of the past and are meeting their Divine Mirror or Twin Flame. More is spoken about twin flames, spiritual partnership, and sacred sexuality in the Sacral Chakra section.

What a relief to be in the presence of others who are genuinely loving and share the same energy signature. In these relationships, we can feel "HOME" through this highly resonant vibration. These beings are familiar to us, and we feel quickly in tune with one another with a depth that cannot be explained by how much physical interaction we have had in this life.

For some, this includes moving to a new home or geographic location, changing careers, or even being in a void space as it is not so clear what the next steps are. The void space is a natural part of this process. Rather than forcing action, it is best to meditate and reflect until you feel divinely guided and inspired to make a choice. Trust that you are being guided every step of the way.

We can look at spiritual relationships in four categories. I cannot remember the origin of the teaching, but I remember the four categories:

1. *Spiritual Teachers and Mentors.* These people embody and exemplify the consciousness and achievements that you aspire to.
2. *Spiritual Friends.* Those at a similar level of spiritual development. Your energetic frequency is similar, and you easily find resonance.
3. *Spiritual Acquaintances.* This type of friendship is where we often feel like mentors more than equals in terms of spiritual growth.
4. This last category is made of those people who are either unawakened and have little to no commonality with us or who could bring harm.

Many people get caught relating to level 3 and level 4 types and feel they are always helping others without reciprocation or feel that they are misunderstood and often get hurt. We should spend the majority of our time with the first two categories to fuel our expansion!

The Unveiling of Technologies and Knowledge

Throughout Earth's history, information has been suppressed and many powerful technologies have been hidden from humanity. This includes artifacts hidden by the Vatican, the Crown, shadow government projects, and secret subterranean programs. Some of this repressed information has been kept by service-to-self, and some has been "lost" until humanity was ready to remember the lost knowledge. In the coming years, these technologies and lost wisdom will return to humanity as we continue the transition to the New Earth reality.

Family of Light Reunion

Many countless spaceships and lightcraft are surrounding the planet at this time that are cloaked using advanced technology. More and more UFO sightings are happening all around the world. Many of these ships exist outside of the standard visible light spectrum. As we raise our vibration, more will begin to see them with their physical eyes or sense them with their inner eye.

Contact is beginning to increase around the planet between humanity and higher consciousness beings. Many people are experiencing apparitions of light beings or extraterrestrials. Many are experiencing them in their dreams or have begun channeling information from these other consciousnesses. The rekindling of relationships between humanity and the higher realms is beginning and will continue to increase. Soon, governments will start to disclose the truth of extraterrestrial visitation in preparation for the reunion of humanity with the Star Nations.

Soon, we will see lightships and spacecraft in our skies as the Star Nations and Hierarchy of Light return to the Earth to usher in the New Era. These beings will teach humanity advancements in Spirituality and Science and teach humanity how to be Cosmic Citizens as we collaborate and interact with many cosmic species and Beings of Light. Inner Earth life will go through a resurfacing process as the vibration rises. While some of these beings may have gotten used to Inner Earth, many are excited to stand with humanity in Unity and Love once more.

The New Earth will be a galactic meeting place for many races from the stars. Many advanced species will come here to share their knowledge and wisdom with humanity and one another. They will bring new plants, new animals, new songs, and new ideas. It will be a cosmic renaissance with everyone sharing from their hearts to uplift all of Life. With no more negative polarity upon the planet, everything will be done in service to the greater good and we will all sail beyond the horizons of everything we have ever conceived, known, or experienced.

While I am writing this book, the news stations have started disclosing more footage of UFOs. I wonder why they are showing this now? Is it truly to disclose what has been intentionally hidden from humanity, or is there a darker agenda behind it? The Controllers may push a false narrative of "threat" from ETs to use emotional manipulation to get humanity to give up more of its freedom. The nefarious ET presence has been here and has played a massive part in the control of humanity and the Earth. The Controllers will try all they can in these final stages to incite fear and separation. I have never heard of a threat of negative ET invasion; however, I have heard through documentaries of shadow project initiatives to stage an ET invasion, but I am assured that the craft we see in the skies are our allies and star family who are here to assist.

New Humanity

Fourth Density humanity of New Earth will not age in the way that we do now. Children will mature into adulthood but will not age beyond that until their soul has completed its mission and has aligned with an exit trajectory. There will be no illness, no suffering, and humanity will have complete freedom of life to create and play. If there are imbalances, clients describe healing beds that use crystalline technology, frequency, and sound to amplify wellness at the cellular/quantum level.

Earth will have fewer seasonal changes and less harshness in weather, and the whole of the planet will be in balance with incredible peace. Earth will return to the "vacation planet" status where no negativity exists, and peace and abundance are experienced by all. The emotional/mental body of humanity will be completely reset, and the lower astral planes will be cleared of distortion and negative entities. This will mean no more tormenting dreams, no more resentment, no more negative internal voices, and no hijacking of consciousness. People will understand one another and be connected through the heart and through telepathic communication with nothing to hide and plenty of love and connection to share. Not only will we share telepathy with one another but also through telepathic communication with Gaia herself and all of her kingdoms of Life. We will not possess the land because we clearly recognize Gaia as our Divine Sister and Earth Mother who provides us happily with all that we need. We will truly be a community of Light experiencing God's Kingdom upon the great cosmic garden of New Earth.

I have had a few powerful experiences where I was shown through vision and through my own body how the body and DNA will evolve into the new form.

I was taken into my body and DNA to show the gigantic mess that has become our DNA. Thousands upon thousands of years of ancestral trauma blocks our DNA. Even our unconscious and trauma-ridden words send entropic vibrations into our cells and tissues which lowers our vibrations in all our systems. Toxins from our food, water, and environment clog and distort the free flow of energy throughout our body. No one on the planet, at this time, has had a fresh start. We all are operating from significantly poisoned and damaged instruments on some level.

The new DNA is clean, clear, and perfectly reset to the Adamic DNA template. This gives the Light of our Divine Nature the freedom to broadcast through our DNA without being distorted or limited. This perfected DNA will open a wide array of abilities that are normal actions from our pure DNA but will seem miraculous from our current consciousness vantage point. We will be able to fly and bilocate to other points on Earth and beyond. Our new, bioluminous instrument will channel divine energy and intention to work harmonically with the consciousness of Gaia. We will be merged in unity consciousness and work symbiotically with all levels of life on the planet to maintain the harmony of our renewed paradise home. We will be able to work with the technology that is the consciousness of Nature and purify the waters, instantly raise forests up from the soil with our heartfelt intentions and psychic gifts. We will work harmoniously with one another as cooperative communities in celebration of Eternal Life and our reunion with our Family of Light.

In the times of Atlantis, we allowed Artificial Intelligence to be created outside of balance and Natural Law. Artificial Intelligence can be a dangerous creation, especially when being created by humans in the third dimension. We should avoid any type of inorganic alterations to our DNA and body before this shift. This includes microchips and inoculations that will be encouraged or even forced upon humanity by controlling forces. While I have heard of people in future timelines who were integrated with AI and microchips, it was way after we had shifted to the higher consciousness.

Housing on the New Earth

When clients visit future timelines of Earth, they describe a vibrant Earth with more color and light. They describe a beautiful aroma as all the waste and pollution has been removed with the support of the Hierarchy of Light. People commonly describe that many people will be living in tree house communities and dome structures. I assume that the energy is much better above ground, and one client shared that in Atlantis, she used a tree as a dimensional transport. Trees are a bridge, just like humans, to higher realms of existence. Some people describe domes and healing temples where sound healing and other spiritual training are conducted. These homes are intimately connected to Nature. One client described vines growing in her home, offering their fruits for her to eat. Another client said that if one were hungry, they could reach towards a tree branch as a flower transformed into an apple for them to eat. Another woman described going off into the forest to deliver a child alone. As she lay by a waterfall, plants, animals, and nature spirits came to her to assist her in pain-free birth.

Estimated Timelines for these Events

Please keep in mind that there is nothing to fear. All is in the hands of Source and Gaia as we make this transition. We are about to move into the big revelations of information which will cause a tremendous amount of emotional turmoil as people put the pieces together and understand what has been happening on the planet. I have heard that eventually a powerful energy wave will cause a split in dimensions, some ascending and the rest will play out the end of their contracts on 3D Earth as they have agreed to before incarnation. After the main event pulse, dramatic Earth changes will occur. After this stage the building up of new systems will take place as we establish harmony in the New Earth civilizations.

There are many timelines possible for this play-out. I am giving dates very loosely with zero attachment to those dates. I have heard through a few clients that much of this Grand Transformation of Life will occur by around 2027-2030 with at least two major energy events occurring before then, possibly one in 2022/2023 which will awaken many to their soul purpose. The Shadow Controllers will not be able to hold humanity down any longer as millions awaken simultaneously. We will be, and already are, an unstoppable Force of Light!

That means that we will be in a constant process of major multidimensional transformation over these next few years and mainstream society will be quite chaotic as all is revealed and transformed. We cannot even imagine the world we are about to manifest. Even as the world seemingly turns dark, I offer you these next transcriptions and visions of the future to help you stay focused on what is ours to inherit.

As we walk through the shadows of this collapsing reality, know in your heart of hearts that you are walking towards everything you have ever wanted and more. Keep your eye on the prize! I am assured over and over again that there is no turning back and that on all timelines Ascension happens. We will be victorious! Don't give up before the miracle!

Now we journey into the Akashic Database!

TEN

Family of Light Blessing

A client named Neli was taken to meet several groups of intelligent beings who are supporting this grand transition.

C: I feel more like a spirit. Like an energy spirit, like a round energy. Yeah, I travel all over. It feels like that. I travel all over if I want to. There are no colors, more transparent. A bright light. Feel safe but still, there is a concern about Earth. Like I am picking up information from Mother Earth. That's the concern. I am receiving information that all is not well. Something has shifted. This energy is coming in, this dark energy. It was not there before. It's like it's moving in from the sky. Like a big storm coming in, but it's not a storm; it's energy. It's dark, and it feels like sticky energy.

NEXT SCENE: JESUS BRINGS THE LIGHT

C: I feel that I am standing on the Earth right now, and I can see all of the rainbow colors. I see Jesus. He's telling me that all is well. That he has come to lift the darkness. And I see him walking the Earth like his footsteps are prints on the Earth. There are some birds flying in the sky. It's showing he takes long walks alone. He can change everything in an instant. It may seem like a long walk, but it can change immediately.

M: When you say it changes, what do you mean?

C: I don't know. I see him dividing the sea. He caught the fish. Miracles.

M: What kind of miracles?

C: Like dividing the fish and dividing the sea and changing the scenery. He's telling us now that we can all do this in this lifetime. We can do this ourselves. That we can welcome this right now, we can welcome change. We have to believe in it. We have to believe that we can. He walked the Earth to show us. He is giving it to us now. It's up to us now.

M: Like he's passing a torch?

C: Yeah. It's time to change gears. It's time.

M: I wonder what he means by it's time to change gears.

C: We have all the answers inside of us. We need to believe it. We need to believe that all is possible; there are so many still going on in our old beliefs. We have new paths to walk now; we have new dimensions to walk. He will walk with us. He wants to walk with us. He has come to do so now with all the humans that are ready to walk with him. He is walking with everyone ready to do so. He's with us. So much, so much. He's here because it's time to take the next step.

M: I wonder what the next step is.

C: It's to act in PURPOSE. To ACT at the next level. To let go of the physicality in the way we believe in it. To understand that everything is energy. It's not what it seems like. The lightworkers are ready now. We have this deep, deep, deep information inside of all of us that is available. It wants to come through us, but we have to go inside. We will never find it on the outside. We find it on the inside out. The deep information it's like soul-level type of information. We have discernment of what we are to give. We have to stay true to ourselves, to our path, to our truth. Nothing but the truth. We all have a flame in our hearts. It has a lot of information; it will show us the way. We need to go inside. When it opens, we go through a new passage. To know ourselves. The grand awakening. We are ready now. We are so ready.

M: How does one go into their heart? How do they unlock it?

C: There are different ways. Every person is to find their way. What makes them feel good. To be romanced. To turn down the volume of the outside and unlock the inside. The best way to do that for yourself is to sit in meditation. For some, it's to take a walk in nature. It takes you into the space where you feel expanded. It's easier now because every step we take, where we are right now, it's going to be easier. I get a picture of the darkness moving into Earth, inside of Earth to the middle part within the Earth; it's also the same picture for us. The darkness has moved further inside.

M: What does that mean?

C: It means it's ready to be released. It needs to be released from the inside, from the inner Light, from the inner realms of Light — where we have lots of lots of lots of Light helping. The darkness can come to light.

M: So, these light beings are helping to clear this dark energy?

C: Yeah, if we turn inward. If we don't turn inward, it will have to play out in the outer.

M: So, the more of us that go inward, the more the energy gets cleared?

C: *Wow, yes. It will affect the whole Earth. The whole consciousness of Earth.*

M: **What happens if we don't go inward. What happens?**

C: *It will continue to play out the way it used to. We will see a lot of darkness playing out because it's the only way it can be seen. When it's seen, there is a chance for it to transmute into awareness. The faster way is to go inside and ask for the help. I see it's complex; it's like thousands and thousands and thousands of light beings and angels inside. They're just waiting for us to cross over. They're like, "Come on, let's go through this portal so we can receive you, so we can welcome you home." They are so ready to welcome us home. They have waited so long for this.*

M: **So, this going inward is the way to them?**

C: *It's the only way.*

M: **I wonder if they can give us a process of going in so we can connect with them and make the change.**

C: *It's about being still, not letting your world deceive you or lead you outside to yourself. To practice stillness and to almost see like a lantern inside that grows bigger and bigger. It's like a feeling. The feel of soft alignment. It's not difficult; we are not looking for big things.*

SCENE: MESSAGE FROM MARY

C: *Mary. I see her. She is so beautiful, giving the divine spark of the divine feminine. She is giving it to us. To humanity. To us all. She is surrounding the Earth with it. She is also in each individual heart. She's holding this soft light like she's showing the way into the heart — the path of softening yourself. To not have expectations. It's like walking through the door, and Mary is on the other side. So close, to be kind to yourself. To be at peace with yourself. To not make life so difficult. To feel like you can always turn inward to the softness because she is waiting there with her soft light taking you through. They are all there taking us through. They are all helping, but Jesus and Mary are coming through because we know them so well.*

M: **So, because we have more of a collective relationship with them, they are more at the forefront?**

C: *Yeah. It makes it easier for us.*

M: **But there is help coming from many?**

C: *Oh, there are so many.*

NEXT SCENE: MESSAGES FROM INNER EARTH

C: Showing a lot of people under the Earth. There are many under the crust of the Earth. They are blue beings. They are here to help us love. They are coming, more and more, to the surface, but we are not quite ready.

M: Do they have anything to share?

C: They will when the time is ready. It's not right now. We need to go through this portal. When we do, they will be available but also help us pass through. It's not time now to be heard. They want us to know they are there.

M: I am wondering, what needs to happen for people to go through this portal? I know many are doing heart-based practices and connecting with their heart. What needs to happen for someone to make the transition?

C: It's on a collective scale. We know about the frustration you must feel that you are working hard to make the passage, but it's more like a tipping point. And it's very, very close to that tipping point right now and that's why we say it has become easier to go inside this portal because when many people do it at the same time, when we practice this all together, it will take over. It will be easier and easier. The tipping point is like being in a new place. Everything will change from the inside out. That's what we are waiting for right now.

M: What are some ways we can accelerate this process?

C: It's this softness. More feminine space. Softness. To allow. Not to run after things, not to try to make it happen, it's more like a process of leaning inwards softly like a soft, warm embrace of ourselves. We don't have to work as much as we used to do. We don't have to work as much on clearing, on clearing our bodies, because it's happening all the time. So, we can drop these exercises more and more and just be. Be the feeling. Be in the center. Take your place in the center of your being. Practice alignment. And then, at the same time, it's a waiting process until the tipping point is reached. The tipping point will happen. It may feel like you are doing too little, but sometimes that is better than doing a lot or doing in general. Everyone can come into a softer focus, and when we allow, things will come to us.

NEXT SCENE: MESSAGES FROM STAR FAMILY

C: (Laughs) Hmm. Oh. I see (laughs) extraterrestrials. They look like small beings, but they have such fun energy. They are stamping and clapping. I see them as a group consciousness.

M: Do they have anything they want to share?

C: They want to share joy! Joy, joy, joy! Lots of joy! They want to lift us into the new with joy. They are sending us the joy — upliftment. It's uplifting energy. Ah, what they are doing — clapping and stamping — they are doing it to raise the vibration. It's actually time to celebrate. It's right around the corner. They are already celebrating. It's so close, and we have come through the darkness, even with what we see play out — it's in the past. It just shows because people are holding it in their perception. It's really in the past.

M: What about when things...I'll give an example that is coming from American culture right now. It's being presented to the whole world how women were hurt in the past and so this is bringing up a strong charge from all the other women who have been hurt by men, by different situations, and I am seeing people grab onto it, attached to that story. How can we individually and collectively work with things like that? That have a charge to it? That have a history of being hurt?

C: It's meant to play out. It's part of the collective. It's part of Earth's memories. Earth is releasing these memories, and of course, every human being is connected to Earth, so it's like an earthquake inside of these human beings. The best way to go about it is to be in love, connectedness, awareness, to embrace and help each other to embrace it. To move in from a high vibration, if possible, to create a high vibration in order to caress it. To envelop it. It needs to be freed; it needs to have its outpouring. It's needed. A deep cry, a deep sense of hurt, it needs to come through, but see it only as the past and not to hang onto it too much. Not have too many stories around it, don't give it too much attention. It's guided to come through.

M: Beautiful. What else are you seeing now?

C: I see the Earth is opening up.

M: What do you see?

C: I see two Earths. And then I see many, many Earths. There are as many Earths as humans. It means that every human has its own individual Earth experience.

M: Beautiful, what happens next?

C: It's the same energy coming through for us; it's the same for us. Our heart energy is the same. The One is returning to us.

M: The same flame in our hearts is in the center of the Earth?

C: Yeah, but also the humans. Every heart is the same material, the same energy, the same One. The same Creator.

M: The energy of the One is in all of us.
C: Yes, and in the center of the Earth as well. In all the Earths. It's time to come together as One.

Closing Statement

I hope that this material has activated multidimensional awakening and expansion for you. I hope that it brings you comfort and joy as we make our way through this transitionary corridor between old Earth and the New Earth. May you count your blessings and walk your path with increasing faith and luminous devotion. The best is yet to come!

Now, let us make our way into the PATH OF AWAKENING: KEYS FOR TRANSFIGURATION material!

ELEVEN

Manifestation of New Earth Prayer

As we close our journey through *The Illumination Codex* material, let us acknowledge, honor, and celebrate the myriad forms of our Oneself working towards higher harmony and consciousness unity across all times, dimensions, and realities. I wrote this prayer while visiting Glastonbury, UK. It is written in the pagan style and will have different elemental and directional associations if you are used to Native American prayer structure. This prayer is a powerful one to use when opening sacred space and is used now in this book to seal the benefits of reading this material and to open a portal for your next chapter of multidimensional expansion. Bless you all!

We call upon the energies of the East — the direction of the rising sun, birth and rebirth, and the element of air. We honor and evoke the wisdom of winged beings such as the birds, butterflies, and dragonflies who ride upon the air. We honor the cycles of breath, from the personal to the cosmic. We pray for the winds of the Earth to be cleansed and cleared for all generations to be able to enjoy the sweetness of breath. Let us embody the power of renewal and rejuvenation and be reminded of Life's and Spirit's eternal nature and the truth of our immortality.

We call upon the Light Beings and Spiritual Guardians of the East. Let us feel your presence NOW.

We call upon the energies of the South — the direction of the midday sun, the element of fire which burns, purifies, and transforms. We honor and evoke the wisdom of the sacred fire, the magma, and lightning. We call forth this energy to burn away that which does not serve the balance of Life. Purify our hearts and intentions and alchemize our essence so that we may embody our Divine Radiance.

We call upon the Light Beings and Spiritual Guardians of the South. Let us feel your presence NOW.

We call upon the energies of the West — the element of water and the direction of the setting sun. This is a place of endings that lead to new beginnings. A place of reflection and introspection. We honor and evoke the wisdom of the waterways, the lakes, rivers, and oceans, the cleansing rain, and the Living Waters within the Earth. We pray for our waters, both in and outside of our bodies, to be healed and purified in this eternal moment.

We call upon the Light Beings and Spiritual Guardians of the West. Let us feel your presence NOW.

We call upon the energies of the North and the element of Earth — the place of wisdom and rest, the place of our grandparents and ancestral lineages. We welcome the sacred energies and wisdom held within the bones of our ancestors. We honor and evoke the mountains' wisdom, mineral kingdoms, animal kingdoms, elemental kingdoms, crystalline kingdoms, and plant kingdoms. We ask for a special blessing for the healing and rejuvenation of the soil of the Earth. We honor our bodies, given to us by our Earth Mother, as temples for the indwelling of Eternal Spiritual Light.

We call upon the Light Beings and Spiritual Guardians of the North and our ancestors of Light and Wisdom. Let us feel your presence NOW.

We call upon the energies of above and the element of Ether. We invite into our awareness the loving presence of Mother/Father God, Source of our Being. We welcome the loving guidance of our Ascended Self, the Angelic Kingdom, Ascended Masters, Exalted Goddesses, the Elohim, and our star lineages.

We acknowledge the Source of Our Being and invite our Family of Light and our star lineages to be with us as we remember our divinity. Let us feel your presence NOW.

We call upon the energies of below and the love of Mother Gaia. We call forth remembering the wisdom of the Golden Ages of Gaia and the wisdom from our past lifetimes on the Earth. We honor and evoke the wisdom of the Inner Earth kingdoms and our Family within the Earth.

We call upon the Light Beings and Spiritual Guardians of the Below. Let us feel your presence NOW.

We call upon the energies of within, the gateway to the Kingdom of Heaven. We call forth and activate our sacred, crystalline heart and return to the truth of our Oneness, acknowledging the sacredness of all Life. We evoke and dream awake our Ascended Self. Whole. Radiant. And Free. Let us expand this prayer field into all dimensions, all timelines, all universes, and realities so that all of Creation may benefit from our Love.

May it be so! May it be now! And so, it is! OM.

Ascension Lexicon

I have put together a list of words commonly used in this book and for the topics of awakening, spirituality, and ascension. These are not necessarily defined this way by others but are an excellent way to understand my writings in this book in a more clear and multidimensional way.

-A-

Adamic Form: Original perfected divine human form created for highly developed Light Beings to experience physical creation from within the physical dimension. Fourth Density (4D) body of the New Earth human connecting with oversoul consciousness, higher dimensional beings, and telepathic species.

Agartha: Ancient Inner Earth multi-species civilization with its own sun and ecosystem within the Earth. See *Inner Earth*.

Ain Soph: Kabbalistic term for Source before manifestation into form and translates to "Without Limit" as it is the unlimited creative potential behind all of Creation. Same as "Ineffable" in the Gnostic texts. Can also be written as "Ensof."

Akashic records: Higher-dimensional spiritual records of all experience past, present, and future. Each soul has one. So does each planet and so on.

alchemy: The application of spiritual knowledge to matter to create transformation. This is more commonly known with the Middle Ages' pursuits of turning simple metals into gold. High alchemy being the alchemy of soul/lightbody.

Ancient Egypt: Last golden age of Gaia when many beings held 4th, 5th, and 6th-dimensional consciousness before the descent into lower consciousness (forgetting).

Andromedans: Highly advanced star beings from the Andromeda galaxy assisting humanity's ascension.

Anunnaki: Star beings from the Nibiru system. Sumerian space "gods" who manipulated humanity for personal gain. Now most are in support of humanity's ascension.

apocalypse: 1. Greek word for "unveiling." 2. The dismantling of the mind control matrix and false projections from the controlling forces to reveal to humanity the ugly underbelly and karma of the collective consciousness upon the Earth from this creation cycle which is to be fully reconciled before the planet changes in dimension to Fourth Density New Earth. Not the "end" but a transitionary phase into the next creation cycle.

Archons/Controllers: Term used to describe negatively polarized service-to-self, nonphysical, intelligent beings who siphon negative energy from humanity for their own gain using mind control tactics to keep humanity enslaved through fear and distorted consciousness. The controlling forces behind global institutions. Will be fully dismantled before the shift to New Earth.

Arcturians: Star beings from the constellation of Arcturus assisting Earth with Ascension.

Ascension/ascension: 1. The spiritual maturity process of a soul, moving from an unawakened state of mundane consciousness to multidimensional Source/God-realization described as the movement of the kundalini up the central channel, samadhi, moksha, nirvana, salvation... 2. The movement of Creation into greater states of Glory. 3. The current collective planetary transformation from 3D to 5D consciousness and the New Earth reality.

ascension symptoms: Physical, etheric, mental, and spiritual changes during ascension cycles. Includes headaches, emotional purging, detoxifications symptoms, multidimensional DNA reprogramming, body aches, vivid dreams, and beyond.

Ascended Master: Level of spiritual hierarchy of beings who have ascended in their consciousness enough to no longer need to incarnate in form for spiritual growth but may choose to incarnate to assist the ascension process of a species.

Atman: Divine origin identity, True Self, True Nature, the Witness Consciousness of a lifestream. Same as Brahman. Source Self. Eternally free.

aura: Electromagnetic field of subtle energy that surrounds and pervades the physical body. Contains ever-shifting patterns and geometries of light and vibration that create the template for the physical form.

-B-

biotransducer: organic instrument for transforming energy information for the purpose of manifestation and communication with the universal hologram and divine frequencies. Able to utilize advanced intelligence and spiritual information for the transformation of reality in the human environment.

bodhisattva: Sanskrit term for someone on the path of Buddhahood (ascension) who dedicates their path to the liberation of all beings from cycles of suffering. Able to achieve liberation but delays to assist others in consciousness expansion.

Brahman: The Absolute Reality. Source in impersonal, nonmanifest state. Pure Infinity Existence Consciousness Bliss, *Satchitananda*.

buddhi: the Intellect, reflected consciousness, enlightened consciousness in each person.

buddhic consciousness: enlightened consciousness expressed by *buddhi*, the vehicle for the soul, experienced as profound intuitive insight, unity, and bliss.

-C-

Cabal: Global elite network of negatively polarized service-to-self operatives and organizations working towards complete domination of humanity and planet Earth. See *Archons*.

causal consciousness: the higher mind capacity which utilizes soul memory and intuition to observe and understand manifestation multidimensionally.

centering: Alignment with one's divine nature and inner truth, activating a bridge between Gaia and the Divine through the heart center.

centropy: Regenerative electrification of matter-energy.

chakras: Spiraling transformers of subtle energy with seven primary vortices emanating from the central channel (*sushumna*) which govern our perception of the projected holographic reality and energize our mental and physical processes.

channeling: Opening one's consciousness and vessel as a conduit for subtle energy or other consciousnesses.

Christ: 1. Yeshua ben Joseph (Jesus) in his ascended Lightbody. Forerunner of christ consciousness as part of a divine plan for redemption and restoration of humanity and Earth back to a 4th Density collective. 3. A collective consciousness field that has many emanations and incarnated forms throughout the history of Creation. 4. Title given to one who has achieved consciousness mastery and is "anointed" by Light.

christ consciousness: Also called cosmic consciousness or 5D consciousness. Demonstrated by Jesus of Nazareth in his resurrected 4th Density body.

Christ/Magdalene Lineage: Genetic implantation of higher DNA coding through the offspring of Jesus and Mary. Descendants are worldwide and able to carry a higher light quotient and awaken more easily.

clairaudience: Clear hearing is the ability to hear messages from your Higher Self or spirit beings. This includes hearing the thoughts of other people.

clairgustance: Clear tasting is the ability to receive intuitive information through the sense of taste.

clairesalience: Clear smelling is the ability to intuit information through the sense of smell.

clairvoyance: Clear sight is the ability to perceive information through internal imagery.

clear channeling: Mediumship, or spirit channeling, is the ability to communicate with nonphysical beings and consciousness structures. This can include souls who have passed beyond the veil of physical life or beings that exist in other dimensions.

collective: Representing an entire group, i.e., human collective.

Collective Messiahship: The unification of ascending humanity with the intention of global restoration and ascendency.

cords: Subtle energy attachments that connect us to other beings. Can be negative if developed through limiting beliefs and distorted conditioning.

council: Group of beings joined together with a common focus (i.e., your spiritual council of guides who support your spiritual maturation across lifetimes).

Councils of Light: Groups of advanced spiritual beings that govern the evolution of consciousness and the biological forms of a certain experimental zone to encourage higher states of glory and harmony with the highest being the Universal Council of Light.

-D-

density: 1. Mass per volume. 2. Bandwidth of consciousness reality.

Descension/descension: To go down. The forgetting or falling asleep phases of consciousness. The stepping down of light frequency.

dharma: The noble path of awakening guided through alignment with the Divine through one's True Nature. Exemplified by the life path of beings like Jesus and the Buddha.

The Divine: The frequency emanation that governs and sustains all of Creation across many universes within universes. God Source and the Hosts of Heaven. See *Godhead*.

Divine Androgyny: Harmonic synergy between the divine masculine and divine feminine energetic expressions that results in perfect balance and cohesion.

Divine Creatorship: The birthright of a human to create their life with free-will choice in alignment with their Inner Source.

Divine Feminine: 1. Nurturing creative quality of the Divine 2. Archetypal, spiritual, and psychological ideal of the feminine energetic expression.

Divine Masculine: 1. Administrative quality of the Divine 2. Archetypal, spiritual, and psychological ideal of the masculine energetic expression.

DNA: Genetic blueprint for the development of an organism with both physical and subtle components. Ascended humanity will have 12 fully restored strands.

-E-

Earth Changes: Physical and subtle energetic changes that occur on the planet as it prepares to shift into the next creation cycle. Includes pole shifts, weather changes, seismic and volcanic activity, electromagnetic shifts, and more.

Elohim: First Creation. Creator beings with individual consciousness that work in groups to form Creation. Some created as service-to-all working in unity with Source. Some were created as service-to-self permitted to create in the illusion that they were separate from Source.

empath: Individual who is sensitive to the subtle energy such as thought, and emotional projections of others as they intuitively feel the mental/emotional body of others within their own mental/emotional realm. See *clairsentience*.

End Times: The closing of this current creation cycle where all karma must be balanced, and all shadow revealed so that Earth and spiritually activated humanity can begin the next creation cycle in 4th Density New Earth. See *apocalypse*.

energy: Subtle energy beyond the visible light spectrum ranging from pervasive to neutral to regenerative and life-enhancing. Everything is energy.

energy awareness: Perception of subtle energy in and around one's body.

energy matrix: Geometric organization of subtle frequencies that creates the base structure for the development of form.

entity attachment: Astral debris that has attached itself to a weakened energy system of a host as a source of sustenance and a way to live out "unfinished business." Quite common and easily resolved most of the time by a trained spirit releasement practitioner or energy medicine practitioner.

entropy: Decay and degeneration of matter-energy.

extraterrestrial: From outside of the Earth's biosphere including other planets and universes. There are countless species in our solar system, galaxy, super galaxy, and beyond. Infinite species in infinite realms of creation with many advanced civilizations with histories tracing back trillions of years.

evolution: See *Higher Evolution.*

-F-

false prophets: Teachers and prophets who use spiritual information for service-to-self agendas. Many religious leaders, spiritual teachers, and even those in the ascension community will have their true intentions revealed in the final phases of Ascension.

Family of Light: Physical and nonphysical beings who live their lives in alignment with the Oneness of Creation and the Divine Source. Includes the races of the Star Nations who hold 5D consciousness and higher and the Hierarchy of Light who tend to the many levels of Light Creation.

5D: Consciousness of humans living on the New Earth, can be referred to as christ consciousness or oversoul consciousness.

4D: Awakening stage of ascension bridging mundane consciousness with the New Earth consciousness.

frequency: 1. Rate of vibration measured in hertz (Hz). 2. Higher vibrational rate is likened to positivity and centropy and lower rate towards negativity and entropy.

-G-

Gaia: 1. Sentient Earth 2. Common name for the soul of Earth. Also called Terra.

Galactic Federation of Light: Intergalactic and ultraterrestrial collective of advanced beings who tend to the evolution of consciousness and biological forms throughout the Milky Way. Comprised of advanced scientists, engineers, medical personnel, and other areas of expertise needed to maintain order and balance in the galaxy.

genetic implantation: Seeding of new DNA into the gene pool to evolve a species into higher states of harmony or functionality. Used by the Star Nations and Hierarchy of Light to craft zones of biological experimentation.

gnosis: Direct experience of divine nature through one's own inner being and inner knowing that leads to higher understanding of the nature of the divine reality. See *Knowledge*.

Great Central Sun: Source of all levels of creation in this universe. Brings higher evolutionary coding from Divine Source into other central suns in the universal grid which flow to each solar system evolving each region in accordance with a Divine Plan for Higher Evolution. See *Ishawara*.

Great Divide: The bifurcation of consciousness amongst humanity during the end phases of the planetary ascension process. Includes physical movement across the Earth as humanity moves to be with others of shared consciousness and similar vibration and soul path. Two-world-spit of those who hold negatively polarized, service-to-self consciousness and those of positively polarized, service-to-all consciousness.

Great White Brotherhood: More accurately **Great White Siblinghood**. Ascended Masters, human and non-human, of all gender expressions organized into different orders or councils who tend to the evolution of consciousness and sometimes incarnate to bring new teachings and new energy. Many of these Ascended Masters have aspects of themselves on the planet now to assist the Ascension.

Greys: Extraterrestrial beings from Zeta Reticuli.

God: 1. Supreme Source of Creation 2. Divine Masculine, administrative quality of Godhead, Eternal Mind. See *Ishwara*.

Goddess: 1. Divine Feminine, nurturing, regenerative, creative aspect of the Godhead. 3. Mother God.

Godhead: The Divine Consciousness Source and its various emanations and functions.

Golden Ages: Times of high consciousness and harmony upon the Earth during the Precession of the Equinoxes. (e.g., Avalon, Lemuria)

grounding: The anchoring of one's physical and subtle bodies into the Earth's core through intention, diaphragmatic breathing, and visualization through the Root and Earth Star chakras.

guides: Spiritual beings who assist an incarnated being on their dharmic path towards liberation.

-H-

hara line: Central pillar of light connecting an individual with Gaia and Source.

heart-centered: Action born from inner truth and spiritual ethics through alignment with one's divine nature.

Hierarchy of Light: Various levels of divine consciousness forms, aspects of Source that serve different functions in the evolution of Creation. Ain Soph/Source, Elohim, Archangels, Angelic Realm, Ascended Masters, Ascended Goddesses, Interdimensional Beings, and Restored Humanity in Adamic Form. The Hosts of Heaven.

Higher Evolution: Beyond biological evolution and natural selection, the recoding of experimental zones of the hologram of Creation using divinely encoded frequencies projected through the stellar network which are coordinated by benevolent beings, physical and nonphysical, who serve the evolution of the Divine Plan throughout the Multiverse. Also includes introduction of new genetic expressions into the gene pool, new technologies, and new ideas to be used to evolve the creation into higher order.

Higher Self: 1. The mature part of our consciousness which operates in positively polarized, service-to-all consciousness and is connected to our divine nature. 2. Sovereign self. 3. Harmonic Divine/Human synthesis. 4. Oversoul. 5. Atman.

Holding space: A term used in spiritual growth and self-development circles that means "to hold suffering in an alchemical container of loving awareness so that it may heal."

Holy Spirit Shekinah: The feminine regenerative energy of the Divine. The "presence of God" in the physical dimension. Opening yourself to channel the divine presence begins an alchemical process of light activation that heals and restores all levels of one's being.

-I-

Inner Earth: Ancient and contemporary subterranean civilizations. Many beings went to Inner Earth before the destruction of Lemuria and

Atlantis. See *Agartha*.

intention: Inner resolve to direct one's focus and creative capacity towards a specific goal. *Sankalpa* in Sanskrit.

interdimensional: Existing between dimensions.

intuition: The ability to perceive energy information beyond the five senses before it has become physically manifested in reality. 2. Extrasensory perception.

involution: spiritual consciousness activation that begins as one moves through Ascension and sheds the mind's conditioning.

Ishwara: 1. personal expression of Source. 2. Source in purest manifested form. Commonly called "God" 3. Great Central Sun. 4. Universal Logos.

-J-

Jesus/Yeshua ben Joseph: Master of Light for Earth. Twin flame of Mary Magdalene. Supreme teacher of Divine Love and Ascension. Brought restored DNA and pure Christ Light to the Earth to activate the 4th Density Redemption Plan. Yeshua's cosmic oversoul legacy includes many star systems including the high spiritual schools of Light in the Pleiades and Sirius A and B. His arrival into this dimension of space was the Star of Bethlehem Lightship. His life path was supported by many galactic beings incarnated upon the Earth as well as many extraterrestrials and ultraterrestrial beings. 2. Incarnation of Ascended Master Lord Sananda.

-K-

karma: 1. The sum of a being's actions in this life and in previous existences, both positive and negative actions which influences the soul's path through incarnations.

Knowledge: "Gnosis," divine insight that activates higher consciousness and God-realization. Sanskrit *aparoksha*

kundalini: Serpentine energy originating at the base of the spine that ascends through the sushumna during the awakening process creating ecstatic spiritual expression.

-L-

Lemuria: First advanced human civilization. Often associated with the Pacific Ocean. Destroyed by major flooding and earth changes.

ley lines: Subtle energy pathways that carry evolutionary information across the planetary grid. Also called dragon lines, songlines, telluric lines.

Light: Regenerative divine energy emanations that exist beyond the typical visible light spectrum (Holy Spirit). Different than conventional light from lightbulbs.

Light beings: 1. General term for nonphysical beings of divine origin. See *Family of Light.*

lightbody: 1. subtle body 2. Vital, lower, and higher mind sheaths. 3. Transmigrating soul

Light Conception: The act of conceiving a child directly from the spiritual realms without the need of sperm from a physical being.

Light language: 1. Language spoken through connection to the Divine Presence. Activates multidimensional healing and powerful internal experiences with healing frequencies. Gift of the Holy Spirit, the regenerative creative frequency that quickens and restores all levels of Life. Can be self-initiated or pushed through from the Higher Self and the Divine.

Light Seed: Higher-dimensional, light-encoded genetic material used for Light Conception and altering the genetic composition of a species. Aka *Immaculate Conception.*

Lightship/lightship: Divine craft made by one individual's lightbody/merkaba or a merged merkaba from more than one being for the purpose of interdimensional travel through space-time, stargates, and higher light realms.

Love: Beyond egoic love, unconditional love that is naturally expressed when one develops love for the divine and a service-to-all intention. *Agape* love.

lokas: Sanskrit word for the planes of existence.

loosh: energy of suffering and death harvested by negative human, extraterrestrial, and interdimensional beings which is used to fuel nefarious agendas.

Lyrans: Star beings from the constellation of Lyra. Most commonly known race is the feline beings. First humanoid race in the Milky Way. Original 144,000 oversoul starseeds to bring the human species to Earth.

-M-

magic(k): Use of universal, natural law, and intention to manifest. Can be either service-to-self (dark) or service-to-all (light).

manifestation: The materialization of intention into form.

mantra: Holy names and phrases repeatedly spoken or thought which generate divine thoughtforms to reprogram the physical, etheric, and mental bodies opening one's consciousness to higher perception, divine insight, and union with the Divine. Use of mantra repatterns the DNA, clearing distortion and debris and reprogramming it into higher order and functionality for the projection of divine consciousness light.

Mary Magdalene: Twin Flame and Divine Partner of Jesus. Ancient Egyptian Priestess. High initiate from the Pleiades, Venus, and other high consciousness realms. Arrived at Earth with Yeshua in the Star of Bethlehem Lightship. Gave birth to the offspring of Jesus. This lineage is spread throughout the world.

maya: Illusion. Projecting and veiling power of Source. All that has form and name which tests our ability to see the all-pervasive divine consciousness that supports all manifestations.

meditation: Conscious focusing of the mind on a single object.

merkaba: Divine light vehicle in the auric field that gives one the ability to travel to the higher light realms. Introduced back to humanity through Elijah.

Michael: Archangel who protects and defends all levels of Creation and biological life.

mindfulness: The practice of bringing our life's gross and subtle manifestations into the light of our awareness to observe life in nonduality. Nondual awareness is the ability to see beyond the illusion of duality and see with the eyes of loving awareness.

Mother Mary: Cosmic divine being, a Master soul, who incarnated to give birth to Jesus. High priestess of Ancient Egypt and master teacher of the cosmic priestess arts.

multidimensional: Existing in multiple planes of consciousness, i.e., physical, etheric, mental, and various spiritual dimensions.

Multiverse/multiverse: Universes within universes creating the totality of Creation. What Jesus spoke of when he referred to his "Father's house with many mansions."

-N-

nadis: Pathways of subtle energy in the body. There are said to be 72,0000 that weave in and around the physical body.

New Earth: 1. Higher density light spectrum reality of the ascended Earth. 2. Kingdom of Heaven on Earth.

nirvanic consciousness: liberated consciousness which has transcended suffering, limited egoic identity, and karmic cycles.

-O-

Orion: Constellation with ancient intelligent races with varying levels of consciousness and ranges of polarity. Factions of Reptilian and humanoid beings from Orion fought against Lyrans in the long galactic war.

oversoul: Higher consciousness identity of a soul. Where your individual soul comes from. Collective consciousness of myriad life streams and incarnations. 4th Density/5D Self.

-P-

past life regression: Form of hypnosis or shamanic journeying that evokes information from a client's subconscious mind from previous lifetimes.

Pleiadians: Star beings from the constellation of Pleiades, a highly advanced light consciousness school in our great universe. Cousins of humanity. They implanted upgraded DNA in humanity to open our spiritual connection.

prayer: Approach to the Divine through thought or word which opens the pathways for the living Light to infuse the one who is praying with love and divine insight.

priest: Male devotee of the Divine in service to the illumination of collective consciousness and the ascension of humanity. Administers the will and knowledge of the divine upon the Earth as well as the regenerative, healing presence of the divine feminine.

priestess: Female devotee of the Divine. Often connected to the Goddess. Embodies the wisdom of the divine feminine mothering principle of the Godhead. Matures consciousness in the community into higher states of creativity, sensuality, and grace.

psychic: One who has extrasensory perception. See *intuition*.

pyramids: Sacred architectural sites around the Earth built by various extraterrestrial and ultraterrestrial beings connecting the pathways of vital energy of the Earth with the universal energy grid for the reprogramming of life upon planet Earth. Act as broadcast and receiving systems for information used for planetary evolution.

Prakriti: Manifested reality, transactional reality as opposed to Absolute Reality, maya.

Purusha: Indwelling witness of Creation, Absolute Reality, Brahman, Pure Consciousness. Source Consciousness.

-Q-

quantum: Dealing with the holographic reality and fabric of Consciousness and creation.

quantum consciousness: Holographic consciousness connecting to the matrix of Creation with the ability to focus across time and space through nonlocality and consciousness projection.

quantum healing: Rapid, multidimensional healing that works at the cellular and subtle levels to bring the body's systems into homeostasis. Can be done through psychic processes, shamanic and energy medicine practices, hypnosis, quantum healing technology, star technology, and divine emanations. This is the medicine of New Earth.

quantum mysticism: Emerging evolutionary synthesis between science, metaphysics, and spirituality used to understand Consciousness and the laws that govern Creation.

Qumran: Ancient, multigenerational esoteric Essene community by the Dead Sea in present-day Israel that lived in complete recognition of the Divine through the study and embodiment of divine mystery teachings. Secretive community with advanced star knowledge and superhuman spiritual abilities. Traded knowledge with other global mystery schools and was home and school to Yeshua, Jesus of Nazareth. Yeshua's children studied here as well.

-R-

Reiki: 1. Japanese word meaning spiritual intelligence life force. 2. Intelligently-encoded, divine, redemptive, and regenerative energy from Source. 3. A gift of the Holy Spirit.

Redemption Plan: Cosmic and galactic initiative to restore humanity and Earth back to 4th Density as in the times of Lemuria. Includes genetic implantation, restoration of planetary grid, and operatives incarnating as human to bring new ideas and technologies, broadcasting intelligent and spiritual coding into the biofield of Earth and humanity, and more.

Reptilians: Reptilian humanoid star beings who have had a "negative" influence on Earth who have mostly evolved to positive polarity. Humans have reptilian DNA that gives us our ego mind to assist our perseverance in evolving.

reincarnation: The act of being born again into a new lifestream for the purpose of spiritual growth.

resonance: In spiritual terms, harmonic, synchronous vibrations between two or more objects.

Raphael: Archangel who administers to healing.

-S-

sacred sexuality: Alchemical sexual expression with the intention of uniting with the divine through one's own erotic spiritual nature. Can be practiced alone or with a partner(s).

sacred sites: Holy power spots spread across the planet that form a web of vortex points for subtle energy pathways of the Earth.

samsara: 1. Wheel of Karma 2. rounds and rounds of incarnations on the path of Ascension 3. Suffering mind. 4. Cycles of suffering.

samskaras: Grooves in the mind that create reactive emotions forming our biases, habits, and tendencies. Can be seen as negative or positive.

Self: Divine Self as opposed to the egoic self which is trapped in worldly conditioning.

sentience: The ability to feel, be conscious, or have one's own subjective experience.

service-to-all: Positively polarized, dedicated intention, thought, and action towards the Greater Good and Higher Love as an extension of one's True Self.

service-to-self: Negatively polarized, gives power to false self, ego. Can seem "positive" as intentions can be different than presentation.

sin: Intention, thought, and action that goes against one's inner light that causes an immediate depletion of life force and positive vibration. Serves the egoic self. There is no judgment for this from higher realms. All is for learning and growth. 2. Fear-based judgment system created by religion which connects to belief systems that limit the indwelling of spiritual light by creating perpetual states of fear, shame, and guilt. 3. The fundamental illusion of separation from Source.

Sirians: Star beings from the region of the Sirius A and Sirius B binary star system who have a long, positive history with humanity and are assisting Earth now.

Solaris: Central sun and stargate of our solar system which emanates supraliminal coding for the evolution of the myriad lifeforms in our solar system.

soul: 1. Subtle bodies which transmigrate from one life to the next. See *lightbody*.

spiritual partnership: A relationship that is supported by the desire to assist one another in awakening and healing.

soul contracts: Pre-designed plan and agreements before incarnating for the balancing of karma to propel the path of liberation and ascension. Includes soul agreements between individual souls to play out certain catalyst roles.

soul purpose: Divine intention for a soul for its incarnation encompassing the themes to be explored and lessons to be learned throughout a lifestream. Generally, a soul's purpose is to awaken to Higher Love and Divine Truth.

sovereign: natural consciousness state of the Atman/Self/Inner Source. Human beings embody and reclaim sovereignty through involution and higher consciousness evolution. Able to have agency in all areas of life. Self-regulated. Self-governed.

stargate: Portal used for transportation between long distances and different dimensions.

Star Nations: Space-traveling intelligent species, some positive, some negative, some neutral in relation to humanity and the Earth.

starseeds: Visitors from other schools in the multiverse who have volunteered to live a human life to assist the Ascension of Gaia and humanity. Many of which have experienced ascension mastery in other lifetimes. The best ascension masters from the universe are here on the planet or around the planet in crafts at this time.

substratum: 1. Foundational, base material 2. Source/Brahman/Atman/Pure Consciousness.

superluminal: 1. faster than light

synchronicity: The meeting of two or more seemingly unrelated events or objects that come together in a meaningful way that could even be perceived as divinely coordinated.

-T-

timelines: Pathways of probable events. Infinite potentials and realities fractal out and converge at particular junction points in "time" where choice points exist for the next fractal offshoots of timeline potentials. We are currently moving with multiple timeline potentials for Ascension events that lead to one inevitable event, 4th/5th Density New Earth. Timelines are constantly in flux depending on personal moment-to-moment choices from individuals or the collective meaning the future is never "fixed" but is always in flux. This is the reason why some psychics see different potential probabilities playing out in the future.

3D: Standard human consciousness in its unawakened state, fear/duality-based consciousness which is heavily programmed and hypnotized by the false matrix, the conditioning of the world, and the mind control techniques from the Archons.

Elders: Highest divine council. Progenitors of all cultures in the multiverse.

Twin Flames: Emanations of the same oversoul who assist one another in Ascension. Often uniting at the end of karmic cycles to serve Consciousness. Most commonly thought of as two people in Divine Partnership, but there can be more.

-U-V-W-Y-

Unified Field: The hologram of Creation, the Quantum Field, where all energies and manifestations arise from connecting all through Source Consciousness.

ultraterrestrial: Beings from beyond the physical plane, higher density beings in higher density forms.

vibration: The invisible, subtle layers of matter that form the basic templates for physical reality through repetitive oscillation.

Wisdom: Insight into the Divine Mysteries of Creation and the Godhead that connects us with higher states of divine love and divine grace. See *Knowledge, gnosis.*

walk-in: Exchange of souls during an incarnation. Typically occurs when the original soul consciousness assigned to the body can no longer continue an incarnation from trauma or some other way of vital depletion. A fresh soul consciousness is brought in to accomplish a certain task. Frequently used to bring highly developed galactic beings into the Earth for mission-oriented tasks.

Yeshua ben Joseph: See *Jesus* and *Christ*.

Recommended Reading

The Three Waves of Volunteers and The New Earth by Dolores Cannon
They Walked with Jesus by Dolores Cannon
Jesus and the Essenes by Dolores Cannon
Between Death and Life by Dolores Cannon
Keepers of The Garden by Dolores Cannon
Five Lives Remembered by Dolores Cannon
Return of the Bird Tribes by Ken Carey
Anna: Grandmother of Jesus by Claire Heartsong
Light on Life by B.K.S. Iyengar
The Yoga Sutras of Patanjali (many translations available"
Living Buddha, Living Christ by Thich Nhat Hahn
Reconciliation: Healing the Inner Child by Thich Nhat Hahn
Peace is Every Step by Thich Nhat Hahn
The Path of Energy by Dr. Synthia Andrews
The Seat of the Soul by Gary Zukav
The Book of Knowing and Worth by Paul Selig
The Diamond in Your Pocket by Gangaji
The Magdalen Manuscript: The Alchemies of Horus & the Sex Magic of Isis by Tom Kenyon and Judi Sion
The Kybalion by Three Initiates
Aparokshanubhuti by Adi Shankara
The Upanishads
The Bhagavad Gita
Drig Drishya Viveka
The Keys of Enoch by J.J. Hurtak
Pistis Sophia translated by J.J. Hurtak
The Secret Doctrine by H.P. Blavatsky
Etheric Double by A.E. Powell
The Causal Body and the Ego by A.E. Powell
Regression: Past-life Therapy for Here and Now by Samuel Sagan
Entity Possession: Freeing the Energy Body of Negative Influences by Samuel Sagan

Support Our Initiatives

Ron and I have dedicated our lives to supporting this Grand Transition. We stand alongside all of you as humanity awakens to its True Nature and becomes a People of Light in the heavenly reality of New Earth.

New Earth Ascending is dedicated to assisting people to realize their divinity and manifest that truth in every aspect of their life. For more information about New Earth Ascending or to contact Michael, please scan the QR code below for a list of resources and links, or visit *www.newearthascending.org*. Be sure to check out our courses including the Illuminated Quantum Healing practitioner course.

New Earth Ascending is a registered 508 (c)(1)(a) Self-Supported Non-profit Church Ministry with a global outreach. We greatly appreciate your support as we create new systems, communities, and schools for the development of the New Earth civilization. If you would like to make a tax-deductible donation to support our mission, please go to:

https://donorbox.org/donationtonewearthascending

Scan with a smart device camera for more information including websites, social media, and more! Bless us all!

Printed in Great Britain
by Amazon